INSIG

EXPLORE
PARIS

WINNIPEG

WN

D0205149

oct 19
2c
1/29/19
u=11

CONTENTS

Introduction

Directory

Credits

Best Routes

ART ENTHUSIASTS

From the big three – the Louvre (route 2), Musée d'Orsay (route 3) and Centre Pompidou (route 5) – to the more intimate Musée Rodin (route 3), Musée Jacquemart-André (route 4) or Monet's house in Giverny (route 19).

RECOMMENDED ROUTES FOR...

CHILDREN

Try boating in the Tuileries or Jardin du Luxembourg (routes 2 and 8), combine the zoo and the dinosaurs at the Jardin des Plantes (route 7) or head out of the capital to Disneyland (route 20).

CLASSIC CAFÉS

Take it easy with the bohemian crowd in the Marais (route 6) or sip coffee like the existentialists at Les Deux Magots and the Café de Flore in St-Germain (route 8).

ESCAPING THE CROWDS

Find a quiet corner at Père-Lachaise cemetery (route 11) or head off the beaten tourist track to the up-and-coming northeast (route 12) or the smart 16th *arrondissement* (route 14).

FOOD AND WINE

The 7th (route 3), home to some of the city's best restaurants, the Champs-Élysées (route 4) for Ladurée macaroons, rue Mouffetard (route 7), with its vibrant food market, or Bercy's former wine warehouses (route 13).

LITERARY TYPES

Pay homage to Victor Hugo in the Marais (route 6), rifle through racks of antiquarian books in the Latin Quarter (route 7) or visit Balzac's house in Passy (route 14).

PARKS AND GARDENS

Take a break in main parks such as the Tuileries and the Luxembourg (routes 2 and 8), or sample less well-known green spaces including the impressively planned Parc des Buttes-Chaumont (route 12).

SHOPPERS

The department stores on the Grands Boulevards (route 4), the boutiques of the Marais and Bastille (route 6) and the bookshops of the Latin Quarter (route 7).

INTRODUCTION

An introduction to Paris's geography, customs and culture, plus illuminating background information on cuisine, history and what to do when you're there.

Paris-Plage brings the beach to the city

EXPLORE PARIS

With two World Heritage sites, 143 museums, over 460 parks and gardens, and 171 churches and temples, it's not surprising that the population of 2.2 million have to share their good fortune with around 30 million visitors a year.

Paris is a comparatively compact city and more suited to walking than many. The city runs for 13km (8 miles) east and west, around 9km (6 miles) north and south, and is contained by the Périphérique, a famously traffic-logged ring road that runs 35km (22 miles) around it. It contains 20 *arrondissements* (administrative districts). The suburbs *(la banlieue)* form two concentric rings around Paris, and are split into *départements* or counties.

Family values

As part of the government's policy to encourage population growth in France, each *famille nombreuse* (ie with three children or more) is rewarded with benefits including nursery provision, subsidised public transport, sports equipment, car tax and school meals, and free admission to museums. The birth rate, which the National Institute for Statistics now measures at more than two births per woman, has been boosted by France's large Muslim community, which could become a majority in the next 20 to 25 years, if demographic trends continue.

RIVER SEINE

The city is cut through the middle by the River Seine, which is spanned by 37 bridges. The river is the city's calmest – and widest – artery, barely ruffled by the daily flow of tourist and commercial boat traffic. It enters Paris close to the Bois de Vincennes in the southeast and meanders gently north and south past three small islands: Île St-Louis, Île de la Cité and, on its way out, Île des Cygnes.

Chains of hillocks rise up to the north of the river, including Montmartre (the highest point of the city), Ménilmontant, Belleville and Buttes-Chaumont (*butte* means 'hill'); and, to the south, Montsouris, the Mont Ste-Geneviève, Buttes aux Cailles and Maison Blanche.

CITY LAYOUT

One of the most persistent images of Paris is of elegant long avenues lined with huge chestnut and plane trees. Chains of broad boulevards encircle the centre of the city, marking where the boundary was in medieval times. Many of the capital's streets contain the word *faubourg*, indicating that they

Time out in the Jardin du Luxembourg

were once part of the suburb outside the city wall.

Arrondissements

In fact, the capital is organised into *arrondissements* (districts), which spiral outwards in a neat snail-shell pattern from the Île-de-France (the 1st *arrondissement*) to the northeast (the 20th). All of these are contained within the Périphérique ring road. When Parisians explain where they live, they typically begin with the number of their *arrondissement*. Within these areas are recognised *quartiers*, or neighbourhoods, each of which has a distinctive character.

TRADITIONAL DIVIDES

According to an old saying, the Left Bank (south of the river) was where you did your thinking – the Sorbonne university has been located there since the Middle Ages – and the Right Bank (north of the river) was the place to spend money. Yet, in addition to this historic divide, there is a marked unofficial division between the traditionally working-class eastern end of the city and the mostly bourgeois west. In general, the further east you go, the further left you will also find yourself on the political spectrum. City planners have been struggling for decades to redress the social imbalance, culminating in urban-renewal projects around the Bastille (see page 54) and in Bercy (see page 81).

POPULATION

Central Paris is more densely populated than London or New York, with its residents squeezed into tiny apartments in the city's 87 sq km (33.5 sq miles). A house and garden is an almost unheard-of luxury, and there is intense competition for desirable living space, with an average of 150,000 people looking for a home at any one time. High rents, especially in the western *arrondissements*, add to the fact that many Parisians have neither the time nor the money to appreciate the city they live in, being locked in a routine that they describe as *métro-boulot-dodo* (commuting, working, sleeping).

Nonetheless, for anyone who is fortunate enough to live in the city centre, the rewards far outweigh the demands. Human in scale, clean, comparatively safe, cosmopolitan and lively, Paris lives up to its reputation as one of the best cities on earth for living the good life.

CULTURAL SCENE

Paris dominates the country's art, literature, music, fashion, education, scientific research, commerce and politics, despite concerted attempts in recent years at decentralisation in France. It may not be good for the country as a whole, or for the provincial cities, but it adds to the cultural richness of life in the capital. Little wonder that the writer Jean Giraudoux (1882–1944) once claimed

Notre–Dame's superb rose window

that the Parisian was more than a little proud to be part of a city where 'the most thinking, talking and writing in the world have been accomplished'.

ARCHITECTURAL DEVELOPMENT

Largely undamaged by two world wars, Paris is the result of centuries of grandiose urban planning. It escaped only by a whisker during World War II, when General Dietrich von Cholhitz, the occupying governor of Paris, defied Hitler's orders to destroy every single historical edifice in the city as the Allied troops approached.

Gothic and Renaissance styles

However, little remains of the city's architecture prior to the Gothic period. The 12th-century west front of Notre-Dame (see page 26) is a fine example of early Gothic, while the transept with its intricate tracery and the interior of Sainte-Chapelle (see page 25) are excellent examples of mid-13th-century High Gothic.

In the mid-16th century, following campaigns in Italy, François I introduced grand Renaissance forms to the French capital. The best example of the French interpretation of the Renaissance style – known as Mannerism – is the palace at Fontainebleau (see page 94).

Baroque and Neoclassicism

In the first half of the 17th century 60 new monasteries and 20 churches were built in the capital, with the aim of turning it into a second Rome. Churches such as Val-de-Grâce, in the 5th, were modelled on the Roman Baroque template with a two-storey gabled and pillared facade, a broad, barrel-vaulted nave flanked by chapels, and a high cupola above the crossing.

French art entered its classical phase in the reign of Louis XIV (1643–1715), notably with the palace of Versailles (see page 90). Louis Le Vau, Jules Hardouin-Mansart and Charles Lebrun designed the exterior and interior of the palace, while landscape architect André Le Nôtre laid out the formal gardens.

The same team was appointed to oversee changes to the city, removing the city walls, replacing the old gates with triumphal arches, and redesigning place des Victoires and place Vendôme as royal squares with statues as centrepieces. The Louvre was extended, and the addition of the Tuileries and the Champs-Élysées created a 'Royal Axis' (see page 30).

The 19th century

The storming of the Bastille in 1789 heralded the start of the destruction of many churches during the years of revolution. However, Napoleon brought reconstruction and extended the Royal Axis by adding the Arc de Triomphe.

By the 1860s, though, a combination of neglect and rapid urban growth had made Paris more than ripe for redevelopment. Under town planner Baron Haussmann, the residential quarter

The Louvre and its glass Pyramid

of the city centre was pulled down, the street system transformed, and parks laid out on the city outskirts. The bourgeois pomp of the period reached its apogee in architect Charles Garnier's extravagant opera house (see page 44), while mercantile success found expression in international exhibitions, notably that of 1889 which brought with it the Eiffel Tower (see page 36).

Early 20th century

The Modern Movement of the 1920s and 1930s and Art Deco, characterised

---

DON'T LEAVE PARIS WITHOUT...

Finding a good boulangerie to sample its freshly baked delights. Buy some still-warm croissants or pains au chocolat and find a leafy square nearby to eat them in. Alternatively, head to macaroon-specialist Ladurée to sample one of its mouth-watering creations. See page 45.

Having a coffee in a typical Parisian café. There are many to choose from and you can make your choice from the historic, and touristy, Café de Flore; Chez Prune, in the trendy Canal St-Martin area; or Le Procope, the oldest café in Paris. See pages 63, 79 and 60.

Seeing the city from the river. Begin at the city's origin, the River Seine. Make your way to the western tip of the Île de la Cité, via the steps down from the Pont-Neuf. From here, take one of the Vedettes du Pont-Neuf boat tours and let yourself be glided along one of the most awe-inspiring river journeys in the world. See page 130.

Strolling in the Jardin du Luxembourg, the most elegant of Paris parks. You'll be in good company alongside joggers, boules players, statues and smooching couples. See page 63.

Getting a towering view over Paris. Climb up the Eiffel Tower for the quintessential viewing experience. If you want to capture the Eiffel Tower in your shot, then head to the Tour Montparnasse viewing platform. If it's atmosphere you're after, make your way to Montmartre in time for sunrise – or sunset – and savour the panoramic view over the city from the Sacré-Cœur's front steps. See pages 36, 62 and 65.

Getting a culture fix. There is of course the unmissable Louvre, but also try and take in one of the smaller, more intimate showcases such as the refined Musée Rodin, the exquisite Musée Jacquemart-André or the cutting-edge Palais de Tokyo. See pages 28, 38, 41 and 70.

Shopping till you drop. Paris is the fashion capital of the world and there is something for everyone here, from the elegant Belle-Epoque Grands Magasins of Printemps and Galeries Lafayette, the avant-garde Colette in rue St-Honoré and youthful fashions and design shops of the Marais to the genteel galleries and passages near the Palais-Royal. See page 18.

Jardin du Luxembourg sculpture

by clean lines and stylised forms, were born in Paris, with architects Robert Mallet-Stevens and Le Corbusier their chief exponents. At the same time, a more grandiose, neoclassical form of Modernism emerged, epitomised by the Palais de Chaillot (see page 71).

Later 20th century

From the 1960s, Paris underwent a transformation. Facades were cleaned, the metro network modernised, and old parts of the city, such as the market at Les Halles (see page 48), demolished. Technical advances enabled architects to build upwards (La Défense, see page 86), expand indoor space (Centre Pompidou, La Villette, Bercy, see pages 46, 77 and 80) and experiment with materials that reflect and admit light.

Eiffel Tower cable car

In the 1980s François Mitterrand left his mark with a number of *grands projets* (see page 30). These include I.M. Pei's pyramidal entrance to the Louvre (see page 30), Jean Nouvel's Institut du Monde Arabe (see page 59), the Opéra Bastille (see page 55), Grande Arche at La Défense (see page 87) and Bibliothèque Nationale de France – François Mitterrand (see page 81).

The 21st century

Recent years have brought Jacques Chirac's Musée du Quai Branly (see page 37), the largest museum built in Paris since the Centre Pompidou, while Nicolas Sarkozy also intended to assure his legacy through architecture as well as infrastructure. His 'Grand Paris' (Greater Paris) scheme kicked off with a pledge of €35 billion for a swish new suburban transport system and he invited 10 world-class architects, including Jean Nouvel and Richard Rogers, to draw up their visions of a more cohesive Greater Paris; new skyscrapers (long banned in central Paris) are already under construction including Hermitage Plaza in La Défense which will become the European Union's tallest building on completion in 2018. In September 2012, a new wing of the Musée du Louvre, designed by Rudy Ricciotti and Mario Bellini to house the Department of Islamic Art, was inaugurated by President Hollande and is the museum's most ambitious project since I. M. Pei's pyramid.

Inside the Musée de l'Orangerie

TOP TIPS FOR EXPLORING PARIS

Nuits Blanches. 'White Nights', or cultural all-nighters, are held on the first weekend in October. Paris stays alive until the wee hours of the morning, with museums, art galleries and other cultural institutions opening their doors for free all night long. Special events are also organised across the city. Some metro lines run all night long on a Nuit Blanche to help sleepy punters get home.

La Politesse. The widespread Parisian reputation for rudeness is largely undeserved; in fact, many locals follow strict rules of etiquette, and visitors are advised to follow the standard. Whether you are buying a baguette or shopping at Chanel, starting any transaction with a '*Bonjour Madame/ Monsieur*' and finishing with '*Merci, au revoir*', for example, should make the world of difference to the service you receive.

Museum Pass. If you plan to visit several museums during your stay, buying a Paris Museum Pass enables you to avoid the queues and save money on entrance prices at over 60 museums and monuments in Paris and the Île-de-France region; you can also make unlimited visits within the time allowed. Cards are available for two, four or six days and can be purchased from tourist offices, museums and galleries, at the airports and online (www. parismuseumpass.com).

Jazz in Paris. On rue des Lombards (2nd) are three of Paris's most famous jazz clubs: Le Baiser Salé, Le Duc des Lombards and the Sunset/Sunside. The Parc Floral inside the Bois de Vincennes has free jazz and classical concerts on summer weekends.

En Vélo. One of the best ways to explore Paris is by bicycle. Borrow one for free through the Velib' scheme (see page 124).

Avoid the queues at Versailles. Book tickets for the palace in advance via www. chateauversailles.fr. One of the simplest tickets is the Passport, which gives admission to the main sites. EU residents under 26 years old (non-EU under 18 years) are admitted for free.

Taking the train to Fontainebleau. The SNCF sells an all-in-one train-bus-château ticket. Check train times before travelling (www.sncf.fr), as services are infrequent.

Vaux-le-Vicomte. You could combine route 18 with a visit to the palace at Vaux-le-Vicomte (Maincy; www.vaux-le-vicomte.com; end Mar–early Nov 10am–6pm; charge), as the two are within 16km (10 miles) of each other and on the same train line. Vaux is the former home of Louis XIV's one-time Finance Minister, Nicolas Fouquet, and generally considered to be the forerunner to Versailles.

Beat the Crowds at Giverny. Monet's house and garden can be extremely crowded with coach parties and school visits so aim for an early morning or late afternoon visit. You can also buy your ticket online to save queuing time (http:// fondation-monet.com).

Rustic cuisine with an elegant twist

FOOD AND DRINK

French food is not all snails and frogs' legs. Its attractions include oysters, foie gras, bœuf bourguignon, steak tartare, coq-au-vin and sole meunière. And then comes dessert: tarte tatin, mousse au chocolat, ile flottante and more.

Paris has the reputation of being one of the best cities in the world for food, with an illustrious gastronomic history. You may not find the most experimental dishes here, and the approach to food is admittedly far more conservative than, for example, in London or New York, but this is not without its benefits, especially for those visitors in search of classic French cuisine.

Vegetarians in Paris

The vegetarian dishes of French cuisine are few and far between but more and more places are springing up in Paris which cater for non-meat eaters. If you find yourself in a traditional restaurant, order two meat-free starters instead of a main course, or stick to simple egg and potato dishes. In an upmarket restaurant, you can telephone ahead and request a vegetarian meal; this gives the cook time to concoct something just for you. Another option is to explore the city's ethnic restaurants, which serve meat-free snacks as well as elaborate three-course meals.

CONTEMPORARY AND INTERNATIONAL

This is not to say that contemporary and international cuisines cannot be found. In recent years, young chefs have been opening more fashion-conscious restaurants – impervious to Michelin ratings – serving French food, yet integrating (cautiously) more exotic flavours, such as ginger, peanut, curry and lime.

The international scene, although not as widespread as elsewhere, is also an integral part of the city's food culture. The greatest concentrations of Chinese and Vietnamese restaurants are in the 5th and 13th *arrondissements* (the Latin Quarter and southeast to the new Left Bank), while Japanese eateries are concentrated in the 1st (Louvre, Palais-Royal and Châtelet).

The best Moroccan restaurants are peppered across Paris, but around the Bastille is a good place to start. There is excellent Lebanese food in the 8th and 16th (Madeleine, Grands Boulevards, Champs-Élysées and West), while good African food can be found around Pigalle and the East.

Traditional bistro

Many brasseries specialise in shellfish

PLACES TO EAT

Brasseries

Brasseries (breweries) were introduced to Paris in the 19th century, at about the time when modern methods of brewing were being perfected. They're a jolly experience: spacious, clamorous and convivial, usually exuberantly decorated in Belle Epoque style. Many serve Alsatian specialities, such as *choucroute* and steins of beer; others specialise in seafood. Outside, you can usually see heaps of shellfish on beds of ice, and men in overalls shucking oysters from dawn till dusk. Usefully, unlike most other restaurants in Paris, brasseries generally remain open on Sundays.

Bistros

On the whole, bistros are smaller-scale establishments and mostly offer variations on a traditional repertoire of dishes including *hareng pommes à l'huile* (smoked herring marinated in oil with warm potatoes), *blanquette de veau* (veal in a white sauce), *mousse au chocolat* and *tarte tatin* (caramelised apple upside-down tart). A number of bistros have a regional bent, and offer provincial specialities such as *foie gras* and duck (southwestern), hot pepper, salt cod and ham (Basque), and *bouillabaisse* (Provençale).

In the past few years, a new breed of restaurant has been springing up in Paris: the néo-bistrot. A response to the economic crisis, the néo-bistrots are usually run by young chefs, cost less than €50 per head, the cuisine is innovative and cosmopolitan, and the atmosphere relaxed. In 2013, Le Chateaubriand (129 avenue Parmentier, 11th; tel: 01 43 57 45 95; Tue–Sat dinner only), which has a daily changing menu with international influences, was voted 18th best restaurant in the world.

Cafés

These, in the traditional sense of the term, usually serve sandwiches, notably the ubiquitous *croque-monsieur* (grilled ham and cheese), as well as a variety of giant salads, quiches and omelettes. Some establishments offer fuller menus with a Mediterranean slant and more elaborate, modern dishes.

High-end restaurants

Whether Michelin-starred or not, this category ranges from the gloriously old-fashioned, with truffle-studded *foie-gras* terrines and venison in grand sauces, to the self-consciously cutting-edge, with hot pepper sorbets to

Food and Drink Prices

Throughout this book, the price guide is for dinner for one person with half a bottle of house wine:

€€€€ = over 60 euros
€€€ = 40–60 euros
€€ = 25–40 euros
€ = under 25 euros

Presentation is of the essence

cleanse the palate between veal slow-cooked in orange juice and desserts that show off fruit or chocolate in five different ways. Such restaurants often have tasting menus *(dégustation)*.

Michelin stars are taken very seriously in France. At the time of printing, Paris had 10 restaurants with three stars, whereas London, for example, had only two, and New York had seven. Losing a star can mean a sharp decline in the number of a restaurant's customers as well as a dent in the chef's pride.

CHEESE

Between the main course and dessert comes the cheese trolley or platter, laden with a delectably smelly array. There are two rules which may be helpful: 1) In a cheese tasting, always start with the mildest cheese and work your way around to the strongest; and 2) Never steal 'the nose' off a piece of cheese if you're serving yourself; always slice cheese in such a way as to preserve its natural shape. This is considered proper behaviour, since it means that the last person served will not be left with just the rind.

The French are the world's second biggest consumers of cheese after Greece: approximately 23.7kg (52lb) per person per year. Many cheeses taste a lot better than they look; some goats' cheeses, for example, are coated in charcoal ash, as this absorbs surface moisture and helps preserve them.

Varieties
The number of varieties means that it can take years to become familiar with French cheeses. President Charles de Gaulle once said, 'how can you govern a country that has 246 different kinds of cheese?' In fact, cheese in France is as regulated a produce as wine, with a

Markets

In general, visiting Parisian food markets is a morning activity, with stalls opening at 9am and packing up at 2pm. Of the daily street markets, the Marché d'Aligre (place d'Aligre, 12th *arrondissement*; Tue–Sun) has an indoor part (the 'Marché Beauvau') with produce of the highest quality (and price), as well as a noisier, cheaper outside section. At the market on rue Mouffetard in the Latin Quarter, look out for the Italian delicatessen, Facchetti, and Steff the baker. Among the roving markets are Saxe–Breteuil (starting from place de Breteuil, 7th; Thu and Sat), with specialists in snails, wild strawberries and foie gras; Bastille (flowing from place de la Bastille, 11th, up boulevard Richard-Lenoir; Thu and Sun), with stands devoted solely to onions, mushrooms, honey or eggs; and Belleville-Ménilmontant (boulevard de Belleville to boulevard de Ménilmontant; 11th and 20th; Tue and Fri), with exotic varieties of peppers, giant watermelons, Chinese cabbages and flatbreads made from rye or barley.

Coffee is served after dessert

Néo-bistrots have spruced up the cooking scene

similar Appellation d'Origine Contrôlée (AOC) classification system, as well as a protected 'Designation of Origin'. There are currently 46 cheeses with AOC status (Roquefort was the first, in 1925), and in total somewhere from 350 to 400 varieties of French cheese.

DRINKS

Alcoholic beverages

It is common to be offered an *apéritif*, such as a glass of Champagne, white wine, a kir (white wine with the blackcurrant liqueur, cassis) or sometimes white port, before a meal in France.

Wine is the ever-present accompaniment to eating, though, whether by the bottle, by the glass or, cheaply, by the jug. In bistros, brasseries and cafés, though often not in formal restaurants, house wine can be ordered in *carafes* or *pichets* (earthernware jugs). Quantities are normally 25cl (*un quart*), 50cl (*un demi*), or sometimes 46cl (*un pot lyonnais*).

The current trend in France is to drink less wine, but of better quality. The interest in organic wine has also mushroomed – Cyril Bordarier's Le Verre Volé (see page 120), by the Canal St-Martin, is a *cave à manger* (a fashionable cross between a wine cellar and restaurant), specialising in organic wines. Recent years have seen a growth in Parisian restaurants focusing on wine, championed by Il Vino (see page 114), which was awarded a Michelin star just three months after opening.

France constantly vies with Italy for the title of world's largest wine producer, and two-thirds of the annual production of 600 million cases is consumed in France; expect, therefore, to find relatively few bottles from overseas on restaurant wine lists.

Beer is usually only ordered with sandwiches, Alsatian meals or Asian food; artisanal beers by the city's first microbrewery, Brasserie de la Goutte d'Or, are sold at numerous bars and restaurants including Le Verre Volé (see above). Cider accompanies Breton and Norman specialities such as *crêpes* or mussels, and is often served in earthenware beakers.

After dinner comes the *digestif*, which may be a glass of Cognac, Armagnac, Calvados or distilled fruit liqueur.

Soft drinks and coffee

Numerous mineral waters will be on offer in most restaurants. Request *pétillante* for sparkling; *plate* for still; or *en carafe,* if you are happy with a jug of tap water.

Coffee in France is usually served after, rather than with, dessert. *Café* means espresso, strong and black. If you like milk, request a *café noisette*. *Café crème* (coffee with milk) is considered a breakfast drink; ordering it after dinner may raise eyebrows. Finally, if caffeine is likely to keep you up all night, ask for a *café décaféiné* (*déca* for short), or for *une tisane* (herbal tea).

Browsing in the Marché aux Puces de St-Ouen

SHOPPING

While Napoleon once branded Britain 'a nation of shopkeepers', nowadays the phrase is more aptly applied to France, and viewed not as an insult but as a compliment for the wonderful array of one-off specialist boutiques and stores.

In an age when shopping seems to be an increasingly uniform experience wherever you are, with the same international groups and luxury labels in every major city around the world, Paris still retains its tradition of family-owned specialist shops, and chain stores and *centres commerciaux* (shopping malls) are far less prevalent here than in most other European capitals.

Most shops open from 9 or 10am until around 7pm. Few stores open on Sunday, except in the Marais and a few on the Champs-Élysées. Some smaller shops close on Monday all day or in the morning until about 2pm. Many close throughout August for the traditional French summer holiday. The main sales *(soldes)* periods in France are January and July.

THE SHOPPING MAP

The city's different *quartiers* each have their own mood and atmosphere, and their shops often reflect the history and type of people who live there. Expect to find shops selling classic and expensive items (antiques and upmarket interior design as well as fashion

labels, for example) in the wealthy, fairly conservative 7th and 16th *arrondissements*, and bohemian designers and independent gift shops and boutiques on the hilly streets of Montmartre (rue des Abbesses, for example), in the fashionable Bastille and Marais, along rue Étienne Marcel and dotted along the banks of the Canal St-Martin.

Couture and chains
The city's big couture houses are clustered mostly in the avenue Montaigne area (off the Champs-Élysées), the Faubourg St-Honoré and St-Germain. However, the once-staid rue St-Honoré has become the focus for a more avant-garde fashion set, thanks to the establishment here of Colette, the original lifestyle store. Even the exclusive avenue Montaigne has tempered its bourgeois image with the arrival of hip young labels Paul & Joe and Zadig & Voltaire; all of which has had the knock-on effect of attracting other cool boutiques and gift shops to the area.

Tradition and change
Emblematic of glamour in the early part of the 20th century, the Champs-Élysées

The Faubourg St-Honoré is seriously chic

nose-dived to tourist dross in the 1980s. Its return to favour at the end of the 1990s was confirmed by the arrival here of *pâtissier extraordinaire*, Ladurée (see page 45), and in the last few years the avenue has been boosted by a swathe of swish concept stores.

In the past decade, designer stores have migrated to St-Germain, much to the chagrin of those who bemoan the loss of the district's distinguished booksellers and literary cachet.

Regeneration is now under way around the widely disliked Forum des Halles shopping centre. After a number of years the Mairie de Paris has decided on a design to redevelop the Forum; a huge glass canopy will cover re-landscaped squares and gardens. The project has an estimated completion date of 2016.

Not that every area is in the throes of regeneration. The aristocratic past of boulevards Bonne Nouvelle and Montmartre is a dim memory blurred by the ranks of discount stores and high-street chains that now dominate the area. That said, the department stores, or *grands magasins*, built in the 19th century, still hold their own and look as impressive as ever.

GALLERIES AND PASSAGES

In the 1840s Paris had over 100 passages, or covered arcades, built with shops below and living quarters above. They were places for Parisians to dis-

cover novelties and the latest fashions, while protected from the elements. Nowadays there are only around 20 left, mostly near the Palais Royal. The passages usually open from around 7am to 9 or 10pm, and are locked at night and on Sunday.

Highlights

The best-preserved gallery, **Galerie Vivienne** (6 rue Vivienne, 2nd), has a beautiful mosaic floor and gorgeous iron-and-glass roof. This fashionable spot is home to the ateliers-boutiques of Jean-Paul Gaultier and Nathalie Garçon, art galleries and the genteel A Priori tearoom.

Galerie Véro-Dodat (19 rue Jean-Jacques Rousseau–2 rue du Bouloi, 1st) dates from 1826 and is perhaps the finest of the passages, with wood-and-brass shop fronts and carved Corinthian capitals. Highlights include leather goods at Il Bisonte and bespoke make-up at By Terry.

Passage du Grand Cerf (10 rue Dussoubs or 145 rue St-Denis, 2nd) is probably the coolest of the arcades – something of a creative headquarters. Come here to admire work by cutting-edge graphic designers, milliners and jewellers.

Passage des Panoramas (10 rue St-Marc or 11 boulevard Montmartre, 2nd) is one of the earliest of the arcades, opened in 1800, and above all a focus for philatelists, with half a dozen specialist stamp dealers.

The storming of the Bastille, 1789

HISTORY: KEY DATES

The Parisii tribe discovered it, the Romans usurped it, the Franks invaded it and Napoleon ruled it. The city's refined culture and revolutionary politics changed the world. The list below covers major, mostly political, events.

EARLY HISTORY

c. 300 BC	Celtic Parisii tribe settle on the Île de la Cité and found Lutétia.
58–52 BC	Paris conquered by the Romans; building on the Left Bank.
c. AD 250	St-Denis establishes the first Christian community in Paris.
451	St-Geneviève saves Paris from Attila the Hun.
508	Clovis, King of Franks, makes Paris his capital.

THE MIDDLE AGES

768–814	Carolingian dynasty. Power shifted from Paris to Aix-la-Chapelle.
987	Hugues Capet is elected king; start of Capetian rule.
1253	Founding of the Sorbonne.
1340	Hundred Years' War begins.
1420	Paris surrendered to the English, who rule until 1436.

RENAISSANCE AND ENLIGHTENMENT

1515–47	Reign of François I, during which he starts to rebuild the Louvre.
1589	Henri III is assassinated.
1594	Henri IV converts to Catholicism, ending the Wars of Religion.
1682	Louis XIV moves his court to Versailles.

REVOLUTION, EMPIRE AND REPUBLIC

1789	French Revolution ends centuries of monarchy, which is replaced by the First. Louis XVI and Marie-Antoinette are executed in 1793.
1794	The ensuing Terror claims more than 60,000 lives.
1799	Napoleon Bonaparte seizes power and is crowned emperor (1804).

Boulevard Haussmann in the early 1900s

1814–15	Fall of Napoleon heralds the restoration of the Bourbon monarchy.
1830	Bourgeois revolution; Louis-Philippe of Orléans becomes king.
1848	Revolution brings Louis-Napoleon, nephew of Bonaparte, to power, and ushers in the Second Republic.
1852	Louis-Napoleon crowns himself Napoleon III: the Second Empire. Baron Georges Haussmann begins an 18-year redesign of the city. The city's first department store, Le Bon Marché, opens.
1870–1	Franco-Prussian War. Paris surrenders. Napoleon III abdicates. End of the Second Empire. The Third Republic lasts till 1940.
1871	Uprising by the Paris Commune, with 25,000 people killed.
1889	Eiffel Tower built for the World Fair. Pigalle's Moulin Rouge opens.

20TH CENTURY

1900	First Paris metro line opens.
1914–18	World War I.
1934	The Depression gives rise to riots and a series of strikes.
1939–45	World War II. France falls to the Nazis in June 1940.
1946	Charles de Gaulle founds the Fourth Republic.
1958	Algerian crisis topples the Fourth Republic. De Gaulle founds the Fifth Republic. Women are finally given the vote.
1962	End of the Algerian War.
1968	Student riots and workers' general strikes rock Paris and force de Gaulle to call an election. He wins but resigns a year later.
1969–74	Georges Pompidou's presidency.
1974–81	Valéry Giscard d'Estaing's presidency.
1981–95	Mitterrand's presidency is notable for his *grands projets*.
1998	France wins the football World Cup, hosted in Paris.

21ST CENTURY

2001	Bertrand Delanoë is elected mayor of Paris.
2002	The euro replaces the franc as the French unit of currency.
2006	New tram service in the south of the city.
2007	Presidential election won by right-wing candidate Nicolas Sarkozy.
2010	President Sarkozy unveils his plans to create a 'Greater Paris'.
2012	Socialist François Hollande elected president.
2014	Paris looks set to have its first female mayor.

BEST ROUTES

Sightseeing on the Seine near Pont Neuf

THE ISLANDS

The two largest islands in the Seine – the Île de la Cité and the Île St-Louis – offer up the full span of the history of Paris, via some of its greatest sights: the Pont Neuf, Notre-Dame, the Conciergerie and Sainte-Chapelle.

DISTANCE: 2km (1.25 miles)
TIME: Two or three hours
START: Pont Neuf
END: Île St-Louis
POINTS TO NOTE: Start very early to avoid the crowds at Notre-Dame.

It was on the Île de la Cité, the largest island in the Seine, that the city of Paris was founded by the Celtic Parisii tribe in the 3rd century BC. The island remains the geographical centre of the capital, though the focus nowadays is tourism, due mainly to Notre-Dame cathedral.

PONT NEUF

The tour starts on the **Pont Neuf ❶**, which, despite its name (New Bridge), is actually the city's oldest. Henri III laid the first stone in 1578; Henri IV inaugurated the completed bridge in 1607.

Statue of Henri IV

As you walk south across the bridge, note the equestrian statue of Henri IV.

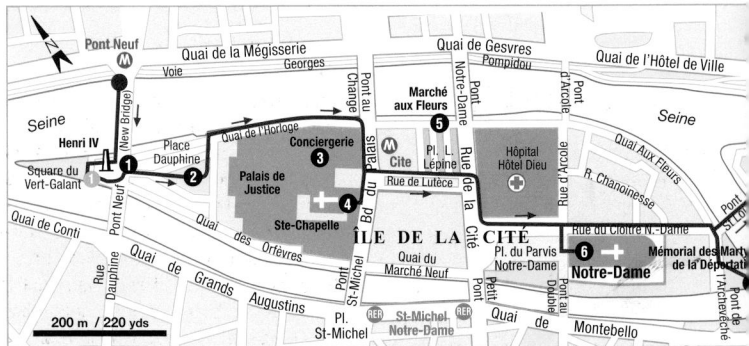

Lunch 'en terrasse'

Originally produced in 1614 under the orders of Marie de Médicis, Henri's widow, it was destroyed in 1792 during the Revolution, then rebuilt in 1818 on the monarchy's restoration.

Behind the statue are stairs leading to **square du Vert-Galant**, a tiny patch with views across to the Louvre and a good place for a picnic. Across the road is the **Taverne Henri IV**, see .

PLACE DAUPHINE

Adjacent to the Taverne Henri IV is an opening on to **place Dauphine ②**. This square was commissioned by Henri IV in 1607 in honour of his son, the dauphin Louis (later Louis XIII), and intended as a market for traders. It is now lined by 32 elegant white-stone townhouses around a triangular courtyard.

Cross the square and turn left on to the quai de l'Horloge, named after the city's first public clock, which is on a tower of the Conciergerie.

THE CONCIERGERIE

The **Conciergerie ③** (2 boulevard du Palais; www.conciergerie.monuments-nationaux.fr; daily Mar–Oct 9.30am–6pm, Nov–Feb 9am–5pm; charge) was originally part of the palace of King Philippe the Fair (1268–1314), but soon became the residence of the keeper of the royal palaces or *comte des cierges* (keeper of the seals), from which the word *concierge* is derived.

The building was later transformed into a prison, and it was here that in 1793, in the Reign of Terror, around 2,600 of the condemned spent their last night before facing the guillotine. Now a museum, the Conciergerie has a guillotine blade on display, as well as the crucifix Marie Antoinette used at prayer when in captivity here, and the lock from Robespierre's cell.

SAINTE-CHAPELLE

Concealed in the courtyard between the Conciergerie and Palais de Justice (the French supreme court) is the Gothic **Sainte-Chapelle ④** (4 boulevard du Palais; www.sainte-chapelle.monuments-nationaux.fr; daily Mar–Oct 9.30am–6pm, Nov–Feb 9am–5pm; charge). The chapel was built in the 13th century to house holy relics, including Christ's Crown of Thorns.

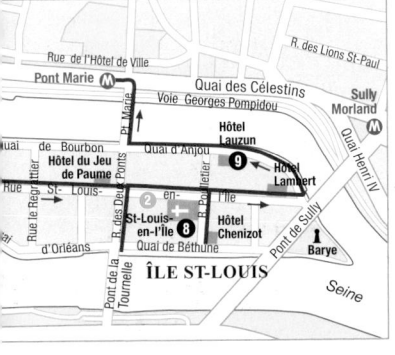

Delicate statuary on Notre-Dame's façade

Enter via the lower chapel, which was used by palace servants. Note the star-patterned ceiling. Stairs lead to the upper chapel, where light blazes through 15m (49ft) -high stained-glass windows separated by the slimmest of buttresses. Those interested in chamber music should check the bulletin boards for concert schedules.

THE MARCHÉ AUX FLEURS

Cross the road to place Louis-Lépine. Here, at the **Marché aux Fleurs ⑤**, flower-sellers ply their trade from Monday to Saturday, while on Sundays caged-bird sellers take their place. Continuing east across rue de la Cité is the **Hôtel Dieu**, the oldest hospital in Paris. Founded in the 7th century, it was rebuilt by Baron Haussmann in the 1860s. Adjacent is place du Parvis Notre-Dame, in front of the cathedral.

NOTRE-DAME

The building of **Notre-Dame ⑥** (place du Parvis Notre-Dame, 4th; www.notre damedeparis.com; Mon–Fri 8am–6.45pm, Sat–Sun 8am–7.15pm; free except Treasury, Crypt and Tower) was initiated by Bishop Sully in 1163, and took almost 200 years to complete. In the centuries since, it has witnessed medieval executions, conversion to a food warehouse during the Revolution, the coronation of Emperor Napoleon in 1804, and the service marking the Liberation of Paris in 1944 (interrupted by sniping and wounding of several of the congregation).

Enter the cathedral through one of the three sculpted Gothic portals recounting stories from the scriptures and lives of the saints for the illiterate masses. Above are statues of 28 kings of Judea – all replicas, since most were destroyed during the Revolution when they were mistaken for French kings.

Inside, 29 chapels line the nave, transept and choir. The rose windows, 43ft (13m) in diameter, date from 1250–70, though they have been extensively restored. The *Pietà* on the large altar at the far end of the cathedral was commissioned by Louis XIII in thanks for the birth of his son and heir.

Treasury, Crypt and Bell Tower

The **Treasury** (Mon–Fri 9.30am–6pm, Sat 9.30am–6.30pm, Sun 1.30–6.30pm; charge), off the south aisle to the right of the High Altar, displays religious relics, robes and jewelled chalices. The **Crypt** (Tue–Sun 10am–6pm; charge) focuses on archaeological finds. As you leave the church, you will see signs to the **Bell Tower** (daily Apr–Sept 10am–6.30pm, July–Aug Sat–Sun until 11pm, Oct–Mar 10am–5.30pm; charge). The 82m (270ft) spiralling ascent takes you to Quasimodo's 13-tonne brass bell and brings you face to face with the famous gargoyles.

Buskers on Pont St–Louis

East of the cathedral is the **Mémorial des Martyrs de la Déportation ➐** (Apr–Sept Tue–Sun 10am–7pm, until 5pm in winter; free), a monument to those deported to German concentration camps in World War II.

ÎLE ST-LOUIS

From the memorial, take the pedestrian bridge to the **Île St-Louis**. Follow rue St-Louis-en-l'Île along the spine of the island past a succession of grand mansions interspersed with boutiques and restaurants. The Hôtel du Jeu de Paume at no. 54 was once a real tennis court. Hôtel Chenizot at no. 51 has a splendid rocaille doorway with bearded fauns, and a balcony supported by dragons.

When you reach rue des Deux-Ponts, turn right for a moment to see the **Pont de la Tournelle** with Landowski's 1928 Art Nouveau statue of the patron saint of Paris, St Geneviève.

Back on rue St-Louis-en-l'Île, you soon come to the Baroque church of **St-Louis-en-l'Île ➑**. Designed by Louis Le Vau in the 1660s, it is notable for its open-work spire, iron clock and 16th- and 17th-century artworks.

Island of Cows

Perpendicular to rue St-Louis-en-l'Île is rue Poulletier (formerly Poultier), once a fortified canal, with the area beyond having been a boggy pasture known as the 'Island of Cows'. In 1614, it was filled in and transformed into an elegant residential quarter. At the end of rue St-Louis-en-l'Île, at no. 2, is the Hôtel Lambert, built by Le Vau in 1641 for Louis XIII's secretary.

Quai d'Anjou

Now turn left and double back on yourself to find the **Hôtel Lauzun ➒**, at 17 quai d'Anjou. Built in 1640 by Le Vau, the mansion was home in 1845 to the poets Théophile Gautier and Charles Baudelaire, who wrote his collection *Les Fleurs du Mal* here.

Finishing the tour here, turn right and cross Pont Marie to the metro. Alternatively, pop into **Berthillon**, see ➋, for their much-fêted ice cream.

Food and Drink

➊ TAVERNE HENRI IV

13 place du Pont-Neuf, 1st; tel: 01 43 54 27 90; closed Sat–Sun; €€
Diminutive spot offering straightforward French cuisine and excellent wines. Try the eggs baked with blue cheese and ham, washed down with a white Beaujolais. Excellent value given the high-profile location.

➋ GLACIER BERTHILLON

29–31 rue St-Louis-en-l'Île, 4th; tel: 01 43 54 31 61; closed Mon–Tue; €
Parisian ice-cream institution (est. 1954) with an attractive tearoom next door.

The Louvre old and new

LOUVRE AND TUILERIES

The Louvre is arguably the most famous museum in the world, with claims to being the largest. There are 35,000 pieces of art on display (from a collection of 460,000) in 6ha (15 acres) of exhibition space, so after your visit you may need to rest on a deckchair in the pretty Tuileries gardens.

DISTANCE: 1.5km (1 mile), not incl. distance covered in museum
TIME: A full day
START: Louvre
END: Jeu de Paume
POINTS TO NOTE: If the Pyramid entrance to the museum is congested, enter instead at 99 rue de Rivoli via the Carrousel du Louvre shopping centre, or directly from the metro. With a Paris Museum Pass (see page 13), you can go in via the Porte des Lions entrance. Tickets are valid all day, which allows re-entry into the museum after a rest in a café or restaurant (or even the Tuileries) outside the complex. Note that entry is free on the first Sunday of the month.

This tour incorporates a morning in the **Musée du Louvre ❶** (rue du Louvre; www.louvre.fr; Thur and Sat–Mon 9am–6pm, Wed and Fri 9am–10pm; charge except first Sun of month and 14 July), followed by an afternoon in the adjacent, finely landscaped Tuileries gardens. If you need somewhere to have breakfast, try the **Café Marly**, see ❶, or, if you're visiting later in the day, **Le Fumoir** or **Le Garde-Robe**, see ❷ and ❸.

LOUVRE BACKGROUND

Originally built as a fortress in 1190 by King Philippe-Auguste to protect a weak link in the city wall, the Louvre was transformed into a royal château in the 1360s by Charles V, who established his extensive library in one of the towers.

Sections of the palace were demolished, rebuilt or extended by successive monarchs, including François I, who in 1516 invited Leonardo da Vinci to be his court painter; the Italian brought with him his masterpieces the *Mona Lisa* and *The Virgin of the Rocks*, now highlights of the museum's collection. Among Paris' main exponents of the Renaissance were architect Pierre Lescot (1510–78) whose finest work is the west wing of the Louvre. In

Capturing famous exhibits in the Louvre

1682, however, the Louvre's period as a royal palace came to an end, as Louis XIV decamped to Versailles.

Artists move in

Following the court's departure, a colony of painters and sculptors moved into the Louvre's empty halls; among them was Guillaume Coustou, sculptor of the *Marly Horses*, now one of the Louvre's most prized exhibits.

During the 18th century, the fine arts academy, which had joined the Académie Française and other academic bodies in the royal apartments, organised exhibitions in the Salon Carré for artists to exhibit their work. This became the tradition known as the 'Salon' and lasted for over 120 years.

Public museum

During the 18th-century Revolution, in a moment of artistic enthusiasm, the Assemblée Nationale decided to inaugurate the palace as a museum, ironically fulfilling the plans of Louis XVI, the king they had just beheaded. Opened in August 1793, the museum exhibited the collections of the royal family and of aristocrats who had fled abroad. These were augmented by Napoleon's efforts to relocate much of Europe's artistic wealth here following his victorious military campaigns in Italy, Austria and Germany. After Napoleon was defeated at the Battle of Waterloo in 1815, many of the stolen masterpieces were reclaimed by their rightful owners, but many remained.

The rest of the 19th century and the first half of the 20th century brought with them periodic upheavals, notably the 1830 and 1848 revolutions, the Franco-Prussian War, the Paris Commune and two world wars, yet the Louvre continued to expand its collections and gradually came to occupy the whole of the vast complex of buildings.

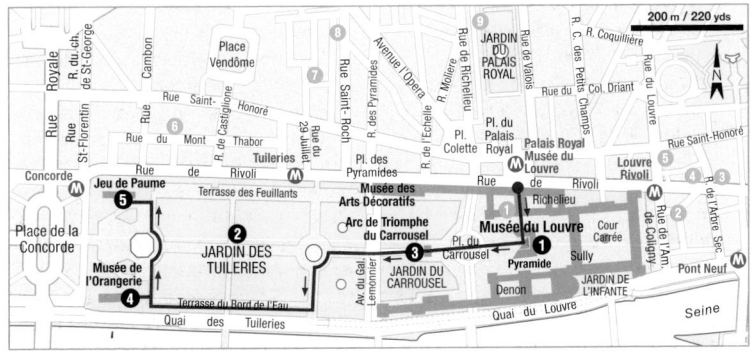

A modern Mona Lisa strikes a pose

Grand projects

The culmination of this process came in 1981, when President François Mitterrand commissioned a massive renovation of the Louvre, as one of his 'grands projets'. When it was finished, the so-called 'Grand Louvre' had doubled in size, giving it claim to being the world's biggest museum, with 6ha (15 acres) of exhibition space. It also became the world's most visited museum, with more than 8 million visitors per year.

The Pyramid

The controversial Louvre pyramid, designed by Sino-American architect I.M. Pei, opened in 1989. For some, it reflects and complements the ancient curves of the surrounding buildings. However, to traditionalists such modernism amid heritage is heresy.

The pyramid forms part of the Royal Axis, or Triumphal Way, an alignment of monuments, regal and triumphal, leading from the Louvre's Cour Carrée via the Arc de Triomphe du Carrousel and Arc de Triomphe to the Grande Arche in La Défense. Contrary to popular myth, its steel structure does not contain the satanic number of 666 panes of glass, but 673 segments.

But the pyramid was not just designed to dazzle. It also allows light to flood into the new sunken court housing the main ticket desks and, along with three smaller pyramids, illuminates the area where shops, restaurants, cafés and an exhibition area are situated.

Latest developments

In September 2012, the Louvre opened a new section to house the Department of Islamic Art. Designed by Rudy Ricciotti and Mario Bellini, an iridescent, undulating roof covers 2,800 sq metres (30,000 sq ft) of exhibition space set over two floors underneath Cour Visconti. The main patron was Saudi Arabian businessman Prince Al-Waleed bin Talal who donated $23 million (£15 million) towards the project.

TOUR OF THE MUSEUM

The museum itself is divided into three wings: **Richelieu** in the north, **Sully** in the east and **Denon** in the south. The collections are displayed in colour-coded sections, to help with orientation, and floor plans are also available at the ticket desks. The following is a brief tour, showing what is displayed where, including information on the highlights from the different sections.

The Medieval Louvre

You start at the lower ground floor of the Sully Wing, where the remains of Philippe-Auguste's fort and keep built in 1190 are on show, as well as some of the artefacts discovered in excavations in the 1980s. Drawings and scale models show the Louvre at different stages of its evolution, and reveal how many transformations it has undergone.

Under the glass Pyramid   *Veronese's massive 'Wedding at Cana' (1563)*

Walk around the medieval walls and fortress, past towers that were once the gates to the city then head to the Department of Islamic Art in the Denon Wing.

Egyptian and Classical antiquities and Italian sculpture

At this point head upstairs to the ground and first floors of the Sully Wing, home to Egyptian and Greek antiquities. The showpiece here, in room 7, is the 2nd-century BC *Venus de Milo*.

For Etruscan and Roman antiquities, make your way to the ground floor of the Denon wing. This is also the showcase for later Italian sculpture, including Michelangelo's *Dying Slave* and Canova's neoclassical *Psyche and Cupid*.

French sculpture

For French sculpture, aim for the Richelieu Wing, where such works as Guillaume Coustou's *Marly Horses* are displayed on the lower ground floor. On the ground floor, the French sculpture collection continues, with works spanning the 5th to 18th centuries. Also located here are Mesopotamian finds such as the black basalt Babylonian Code of Hammurabi (1792–1750 BC), which is one of the world's first legal documents.

French masterpieces

The first floor exhibits some of the Western world's most iconic images. In the Denon Wing are some spectacular large-format French paintings, notably Eugène Delacroix's *Liberty Leading the People*, Théodore Géricault's *Raft of the Medusa* and Jacques-Louis David's *Consecration of Napoleon*. This last picture shows the scene in Notre-Dame at which Napoleon is said to have snubbed the Pope and crowned himself emperor, before crowning Josephine too. There are good views of the roof of the new Department of Islamic Art from the Salle des Etats.

Mona Lisa

Adjacent in Room 6 is Leonardo da Vinci's enigmatic Florentine noblewoman, the *Mona Lisa* (entitled *La Joconde*, in French, after the name of her husband: Francesco del Giocondo). This

The *Venus de Milo*

With her serene gaze, soft curves and naturalistic drapery, the Venus de Milo was discovered, minus her arms, on the island of Milos in 1820 and promptly purchased by the French government for 6,000 francs. The sensuous statue has been identified as Aphrodite, the Greek goddess of love and beauty, who is often represented half naked, and was probably inspired by the works of Praxiteles. Working in the mid-4th century BC, the Greek sculptor was a forerunner of Hellenistic art, and his nude interpretations of gods and goddesses were often copied.

Palatial decor

16th-century portrait was bought into France by François I, when the artist came to work at his court; in the 1980s it was attacked and is therefore now protected by bullet-proof glass. It was also famously stolen by an Italian patriot in 1911, but was thankfully returned in 1914. Hanging alongside is Paolo Veronese's *Wedding at Cana*, where Jesus is said to have turned water into wine.

Other first-floor highlights

At the staircase dividing the Denon and Sully wings is the *Winged Victory of Samothrace* (2nd century BC), a Hellenistic figurehead commemorating a victory at sea, and the glittering Galerie d'Apollon (Apollo's Gallery), which holds the crown jewels. Note also the gallery's elaborate ceiling by Eugène Delacroix. The first floor of the Richelieu Wing contains Napoleon III's apartments, which now display works of the decorative arts.

French and Dutch painting

The whole of the second floor is devoted to painting, with highlights including Dürer's *Self-Portrait*, Vermeer's *The Lacemaker*, Watteau's *Pierrot* and Ingres' *The Turkish Bath*. Look out for the Rubens Room, devoted to the 24 pictures produced between 1622 and 1625 for Marie de Médicis, illustrating the principal events in her life.

The Richelieu Wing houses works from Flanders, Holland/The Netherlands and Germany (14th to 17th centuries), while the second floor of Sully is devoted to French paintings of the 17th, 18th and 19th centuries.

Other museums

In a separate wing of the Louvre (entrance at 107 rue de Rivoli, www. lesartsdecoratifs.fr; Tue–Wed and Fri–Sun 11am–6pm,Thu until 9pm; charge) are three other collections, covering the decorative arts, fashion and textiles, and advertising. The **Musée des Arts Décoratifs** presents a survey of interior design from medieval tapestries to 21stcentury design. The **Musée des Arts de la Mode et du Textile** covers Paris fashions and textiles from the 16th century to the present, and the **Musée de la Publicité** exhibits advertising paraphernalia from the Middle Ages to the present day.

Break for lunch

At this point, you'll probably be firmly in need of refreshment. Options in the vicinity of the Louvre include **Chez la Vieille – Adrienne,** see ④; **Kaï**, see ⑤; **L'Ardoise**, see ⑥; **Le Rubis**, see ⑦; **La Ferme Opéra**, see ⑧; and the **Bar de l'Entr'acte**, see ⑨.

The Tuileries

Once sated, head directly west of the pyramid for a stroll round the **Jardin des Tuileries** ❷ (rue de Rivoli, 1st; daily 7.30am–7pm; free). Once a rubbish tip and clay quarry for tiles (*tuiles,*

The beautiful Tuileries

The ever-popular Mona Lisa

hence the name), the garden was created in 1564 for Catherine de Médicis in front of what was then the Palais des Tuileries (see page 33). The Italian-style garden was intended to remind her of her native Tuscany.

Public park

In 1664, Louis XIV's landscape gardener, André Le Nôtre, redesigned the park with his predilection for straight lines and clipped trees. It was opened to the public and became the first fashionable outdoor area in which to see and be seen, prompting the addition of the first deckchairs and public toilets.

In the 1990s the gardens were renovated, reinstating Le Nôtre's original design and incorporating a new sloping terrace and enclosed garden. The Passerelle Léopold-Sédar-Senghor, a footbridge across the Seine opened in 1999, links the southwestern corner of the gardens to the Left Bank.

Arc de Triomphe du Carrousel

Approaching the gardens from the Louvre, you pass through the **Arc de Triomphe du Carrousel** ❸, which is the smallest of the three arches on the Royal Axis. Erected in 1808 by Napoleon to commemorate his Austrian victories, the pink arch is a rather garish imitation of the triumphal arches built by the Romans, and the four galloping horses on top are copies of four gilded bronze horses, stolen by Napoleon from St Mark's Square in Venice to decorate this memorial. After the emperor's downfall in 1815, the originals were returned.

Sculpture garden

In front of the arch, where the Tuileries Palace once stood, is a group of sculptures of sensuous nudes, created between 1900 and 1938 by Aristide Maillol to adorn the ornamental pools. Numerous other sculptures decorate the gardens, including works by Marly, Le Paultre and Coustou, who were among the first artists to work in

The lost palace

In between the Louvre and the Tuileries Garden was once another palace. Originally built by Catherine de Médicis in the 1560s, it was later occupied by Louis XIV while he waited for Versailles to be built. In the Revolution, however, Louis XVI and Marie Antoinette were forced back to the Tuileries from Versailles and held under house arrest there. The palace was stormed and looted by the mob, leaving over 1,000 corpses strewn around the complex; the king and queen took refuge with the Legislative Assembly. The palace was attacked twice more by revolutionaries, in 1830 and 1848, only to be restored, and then finally burned in 1871 during the Paris Commune, as a symbol of the former royal and imperial regimes.

Sitting by the hexagonal pool

the Louvre after Louis XIV abandoned it for Versailles. There are also works by much later artists, including Rodin, Jean Dubuffet, Ellsworth Kelly and David Smith.

Hexagonal pool

At this point continue westwards along the Terrasse du Bord de l'Eau, where Napoleon's children played under the watchful gaze of their father, to the **hexagonal pool** – still a favourite spot for children with boats. There are usually plenty of chairs around here, if you are in need of a rest and even a snooze.

THE ORANGERIE

In the southwest corner of the Tuileries is the **Musée de l'Orangerie ❹** (www. musee-orangerie.fr; Wed–Mon 9am–6pm; charge).

Waterlilies

The building was constructed as a hot-house by Napoleon III, but since the 1920s has been the showcase for eight massive canvases of waterlilies, *Les Nymphéas,* by Claude Monet. In these works, the Impressionist painter captured the play of light and colour on the pond in his garden at Giverny (see page 96) at different times of day, and in doing so caught a dream-like feeling of infinite space. Extensively renovated and reopened in 2006, the two elegant oval rooms upstairs dis-play the paintings as originally pre-scribed by Monet himself.

Basement Gallery

In the gallery space downstairs is the **Jean Walter and Paul Guillaume Collection**, with high-quality examples of the work of Cézanne, Renoir, Matisse, Picasso, Soutine, Modigliani, Utrillo, Henri Rousseau and others.

JEU DE PAUME

With place de la Concorde on your left, walk to the **Jeu de Paume ❺**, in the northwest corner of the Tuileries. The building was originally constructed in 1861 to house real-tennis courts (hence the name, which means real tennis in French), though it soon became an art museum. From 1940 to 1944 the Jeu de Paume was used to store artworks stolen from French Jews by the Nazi regime. The museum's curator, Rose Valland, a member of the Resistance, notified her fellow *résistants* about which trains contained France's art treasures, so they would not blow them up.

Centre National de la Photographie

The building now houses the stylish **Centre National de la Photographie** (www.jeudepaume.org; Tue 11am–9pm, Wed–Sun until 7pm; charge), which puts on exhibitions of all photographic disciplines, including major fashion retrospectives and contemporary video installations.

Monet's 'Waterlilies' in the Orangerie

Food and Drink

① CAFÉ MARLY

93 rue de Rivoli, cour Napoléon du Louvre, 1st; daily 8am–2am; tel: 01 49 26 06 60; €€€€

Open all day every day and particularly good for breakfast. Sit on the terrace overlooking the glass pyramid or enjoy the plush interior.

② LE FUMOIR

6 rue de l'Amiral-de-Coligny, 1st; tel: 01 42 92 00 24; daily 11am–2am; €€€

This 'smoking room' feels more like a club than a bar. Regulars sit in squishy leather seats while sipping Mojitos and perusing something from the 3,000-plus library.

③ LE GARDE-ROBE

41 rue de l'Arbre Sec, 1st; tel: 01 49 26 90 60; closed Sat lunch and Sun; €–€€

The 'wardrobe' is a tiny bar with two acclaimed sommeliers, Nathalie and Robin. There are around 200 different wines here, most of which are available by the glass. Food is available in the form of platters of cheese, charcuterie or oysters.

④ CHEZ LA VIEILLE – ADRIENNE

1 rue Bailleul, 1st; tel: 01 42 60 15 78, closed Sat lunch and Sun; €€€

Classic bistro with good food in homely portions. The Corsican owner will eulogise about his tripe and *pot-au-feu*, then talk at length on his various desserts.

⑤ KAÏ

18 rue du Louvre, 1st; tel: 01 40 15 01 99; closed Sun; €€€€

One of many excellent (and pricey) Japanese restaurants near the museum but this one has value-for-money lunch menus starting at €25. Desserts, to die for, are from Pierre Hermé.

⑥ L'ARDOISE

28 rue du Mont Thabor, 1st; tel: 01 42 96 28 18; closed Sun lunch and Mon; €€€

Excellent food from chef Pierre Jay. Unlike many bistros it opens on Sunday evening.

⑦ LE RUBIS

10 rue du Marché-St-Honoré, 1st; tel: 01 42 61 03 34; closed Sun; €

Wine bar with rustic *plats du jour* such as sausages with lentils. Food is served at lunch only, but the bar functions from 12-10.30pm.

⑧ LA FERME OPÉRA

55–7 rue St-Roch, 1st; tel: 01 40 20 12 12; open daily; €€

Self-service deli with healthy salads, sandwiches, fruit juices, cakes and tarts. Good-quality ingredients.

⑨ BAR DE L'ENTR'ACTE

47 rue de Montpensier, 1st; tel: 01 42 97 57 76; €

In an otherwise chic area, this tiny bar has shabby appeal. Serves simple snacks throughout the day.

The iconic Eiffel Tower

THE 7TH

The 7th arrondissement has some of the city's grandest monuments set amongst wide avenues, lofty mansions, ministries and embassies. Most impressive of all is that most iconic of Parisian – and French – symbols: the Eiffel Tower.

> **DISTANCE:** 4.5km (2.75 miles)
> **TIME:** A full day
> **START:** Tour Eiffel (Eiffel Tower)
> **END:** Musée d'Orsay
> **POINTS TO NOTE:** Consider doing this tour on a Thursday, when the Musée d'Orsay has a late closing time of 9.45pm. At the start, expect queues at the Eiffel Tower, which is always busy.

Whichever direction you approach it from, you can't miss the **Tour Eiffel ①** (Eiffel Tower; Champs de Mars; www.tour-eiffel.fr; daily Sept–mid-June 9.30am–11.45pm for lifts, 9.30am–6.30pm steps only, mid-June–Aug 9am–12.45am for lifts and steps, last lift 45 min before closing; charge). At 300m (985ft), the tower is still the city's tallest structure and the world's most visited paid monument.

History

The tower was built according to plans by architect Gustave Eiffel between 28 January 1887 and 31 March 1889 for the Paris Universal Exhibition of 1889 and was intended to stand for only 20 years. Initially, the reception to the tower was frosty, but the advent of radio and the tower's usefulness as a site for antennae secured its future. Even so, it survived a lightning strike in 1902, being 'sold' twice for scrap by a con artist in 1925, a demolition order from Hitler as the Allies neared Paris in 1944, and the ravages of corrosion: tons of rust were removed during its 100th birthday facelift. The tower has been repainted 19 times, each time requiring 60 tonnes of paint and taking around 18 months.

First and second platforms

The first platform is 57m (187ft) up, while the second level is at 115m (377ft). In total, there are 1,652 steps. The standard way to ascend is either on foot or in the glass-walled elevators, for which there are always long queues. At the time of writing, the first floor was undergoing a facelift, including the installation of some glass flooring (gulp!) and a new museum.

The view from below...   *...and from the top*

One way of avoiding the queues is to go for a meal at the gourmet **Jules Verne** restaurant, on the second platform (booking essential on tel: 01 45 55 61 44), for which there is a private elevator. You pay a premium for this, but the views are unbeatable.

Third platform

From the second platform, the only way up is by elevator, which means further queuing. This takes visitors to the third level, 300m (985ft) up, from which there are views for approximately 65km (40 miles) on a clear day. The platform on the third level is glazed, and there are signs indicating which sights are which. Also on this level is Gustave Eiffel's office, modelled as it would have been in his day, and the rather more recent addition of a champagne bar (noon–10pm).

Although the tower has restaurants, the **Café Constant**, see ①, in a nearby street below, is a great option for lunch.

QUAI BRANLY

After lunch, you may wish to see the city's newest museum, the **Musée du Quai Branly** ② (37 quai Branly; www.quai branly.fr; Tue, Wed, Sun 11am–7pm, Thur–Sat 11am–9pm; charge). To reach it, head east from the Eiffel Tower. The anthropology museum opens a window on to cultures as diverse as those of the Pacific Islands and Africa.

CHAMPS DE MARS

Now returning to the Eiffel Tower, walk up through the **Champs de Mars** ③. Once a military parade ground, it stretches away from the river, ironically, via the glass Wall for Peace, up to the **École Militaire**, France's officer-training academy. Napoleon famously graduated from here in just one year instead of two. Turn left on avenue de la Motte Picquet to place de l'École Militaire, then take the 45-degree turn on to avenue de Tourville, where the **Hôtel des Invalides** ④ is on your left at place Vauban.

LES INVALIDES

The building of a home and hospital for aged and wounded soldiers was initiated by Louis XIV in 1670 using Libéral Bruant, and later Hardouin Mansart, as architects. It once housed 6,000 invalids. Now, part is still a hospital; the rest a museum of military history.

There is also a chapel for the veterans and a separate royal chapel, the **Église du Dôme** (129 rue de Grenelle, 7th; www.invalides.org; daily Nov–Mar 10am–5pm Apr–Oct 10am–6pm also Apr–Sept Tue until 9pm, July–Aug dome open until 7pm; closed first Sun of month; charge), with a gilded dome guarding Napoleon's lavish tomb.

The **Musée de l'Armée** (details same as for the Église du Dôme; charge) comprises the royal armoury (from which, in 1789, revolutionaries commandeered

Musée Rodin's exquisite garden

30,000 rifles for storming the Bastille), a fine collection of paintings (note Ingres' *Emperor Napoleon on the Throne*), and sections on the two world wars.

MUSÉE RODIN

As you leave Les Invalides turn left on boulevard des Invalides, cross over and then turn right at rue de Varenne. On your right is the **Musée Rodin 5** (79 rue de Varenne; www.musee-rodin. fr; Tue, Thu–Sun 10am–5.45pm, Wed until 8.45pm, Oct–Mar garden closes at 5pm; charge).

The museum is housed in the Hôtel de Biron, built in 1728. Rodin moved here in 1908 and struck a deal with the government to bequeath all his works to the state on condition that they would be exhibited in the house and park.

Highlights

As you approach the house, you will find Rodin's famous statue, *The Thinker*, set high up amongst the greenery. Once inside, the decor is bare but elegant. As well as Rodin's works on display here, there are also paintings by Van Gogh, Monet and Renoir, and sculptures by Camille Claudel, Rodin's assistant and mistress. The beautiful gardens behind the house are populated with more of Rodin's statues, and there is also a

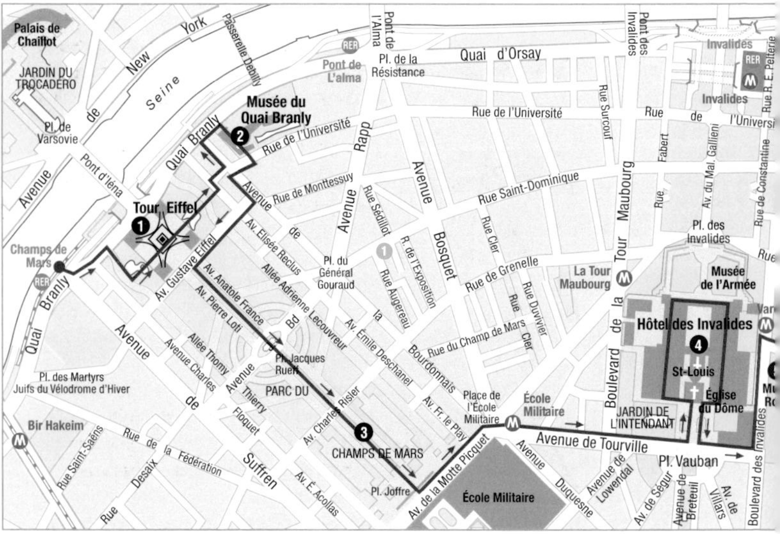

Musée d'Orsay's central aisle   *Orsay's Café Campana*

café. At the time of writing, the museum was only partially open while undergoing renovations, which were due to be completed in 2014.

MUSÉE D'ORSAY

Continue down rue de Varenne then turn left at rue de Bellechasse. If you overshoot the turning, on your right on rue de Varenne is the **Hôtel Matignon**, the residence of the French prime minister. Following rue de Bellechasse to the river, you come to the **Musée d'Orsay ❻** (1 rue de la Légion d'Honneur; quai Anatole France; www.musee-orsay.fr; Tue–Sun 9.30am–6pm, Thu until 9.45pm; charge).

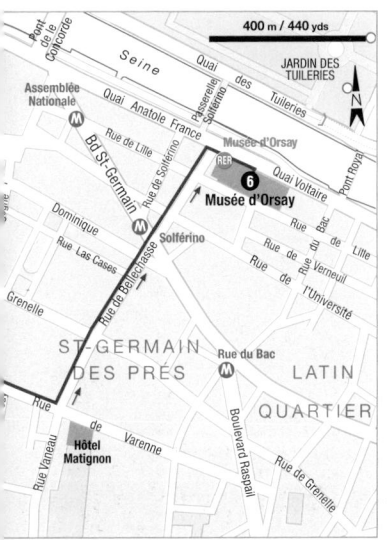

This art museum was originally a railway station, built for the Universal Exhibition of 1900. It was subsequently used as a prisoner of war depot during World War II, a set for several films, and then an auction house, before finally becoming a museum in the 1980s.

Exhibits

Dedicated to art from 1848 to 1914, the galleries are organised roughly chronologically. On the ground floor, where trains from southwest France once puffed in, you are taken from Delacroix and Corot up to the birth of Impressionism with early Monet and Renoir. On the mezzanine floor are sections on Art Nouveau design, paintings by neo and Post-Impressionists including Van Gogh, and sculpture by Maillol and Rodin. There is also a restaurant with an exuberant Belle Epoque interior. On the top level, which is often crowded, are the Impressionists, notably Manet, Monet, Degas, Renoir and Cézanne. Check out the views over the Seine from the terrace.

Food and Drink

❶ LE CAFÉ CONSTANT

139 rue St-Dominique, 7th; tel: 01 47 53 73 34; Tue–Sun; €€€

At this fashionable café-bistro, with a zinc bar and blackboard menu, chef Christian Constant produces traditional dishes in modern style.

The imposing Arc de Triomphe

CHAMPS-ÉLYSÉES AND GRANDS BOULEVARDS

This route covers some of the city's smartest avenues, squares and shops, and some big, bold attractions: from the monumental Arc de Triomphe to the Belle Epoque Grand and Petit Palais, and the capital's historic department stores.

DISTANCE: 4.75km (3 miles)
TIME: A full day
START: Arc de Triomphe
END: Palais Royal
POINTS TO NOTE: This is a fairly long route, so consider taking the green no. 73 bus down the Champs-Élysées after visiting the Arc de Triomphe. Book in advance for the Grand Palais to avoid the queues.

There is a lot to take in on this route, so you might consider doing it in two halves: the Arc de Triomphe to place de la Concorde, and the Madeleine to the Palais Royal.

ARC DE TRIOMPHE

At metro Charles-de-Gaulle-Étoile, take the subway to access the centre of the roundabout, amidst a chaotic whirl of cars (prangs here are specifically excluded from most insurance policies). In the middle is the **Arc de Triomphe ❶**

(place Charles-de-Gaulle; www.arc-de-triomphe.monuments-nationaux.fr; daily Apr–Sept 10am–11pm, Oct–Mar 10am–10.30pm; lift for disabled visitors; charge), begun by Napoleon in 1806 but not completed until 30 years later under King Louis Philippe.

It commemorates Napoleon's army and is decorated with reliefs of famous victories. On the right (with your back to the Champs-Élysées) is the *Marseillaise*, sculpted by François Rude and representing 'Nation' leading the French into combat for the country's freedom. Under the arch is the *Tomb of the Unknown Soldier*, sited here in 1920 and with a flame of remembrance kept constantly alight.

From the top of the monument you can enjoy a spectacular view of the 12 avenues that radiate from l'Étoile (meaning 'of the star'), as the square is generally known. It was the 'other' Napoleon (Bonaparte's nephew, known to some as 'Napoleon the Little'), who, together with the Prefect of Paris, Baron Haussmann, created these wide boulevards flanked by chestnut trees.

Louis Vuitton's flagship store on the Champs

CHAMPS-ÉLYSÉES

First initiated by Louis XVI in 1667, the **Champs-Élysées**, or 'Elysian Fields' were laid out by landscape architect André Le Nôtre as an extension of the Jardin des Tuileries, running west from the Louvre. During the Second Empire (1852–70) the avenue gave way to sumptuous hotels, chic shops and desirable corporate addresses. In 1871, Bismark's Prussian troops marched up here in triumph, and in 1940 Hitler's did likewise. Today, however, the avenue is home to cinemas, restaurants and the swanky flagship stores of large chains.

Between the top end of the avenue and the **Rond-Point** ❷ at the halfway stage, you pass the high-class Four Seasons **Hotel George V** on the avenue of the same name on your right and the Guerlain perfume store, with its opulent interior, on your left at no. 68. The first right turn off the Rond-Point is **avenue Montaigne**, where many leading fashion houses, including Céline, Chanel, Christian Dior and Prada have flagship stores.

After the Rond-Point, on your right (before the Grand and Petit Palais) is the **Théâtre du Rond-Point**, with its stylish interior (and bar). Meanwhile, on your left is the **Palais de l'Élysée**, the president's residence, down avenue de Marigny. **Ladurée**, see ❶, is worth a stop for cake-tastic refreshments.

If you're feeling up to it and want to visit a charming little museum, take a slight detour off our route, walk all the way up avenue Franklin-Roosevelt until you reach boulevard Haussmann. At No. 158, the **Musée Jacquemart-André** (www.musee-jacquemart-andre.com; daily 10am–6pm; charge) houses a collection of art and furniture that once belonged to wealthy collector Edouard André and his wife, erstwhile portrait painter, Nélie Jacquemart. Highlights include works by Boucher, Rembrandt and Titian, as well as a wonderfully sumptuous dining room (11.45am– 5.30pm) with a trompe l'oeil ceiling by Tiepolo, vast windows and delicious cakes.

GRAND AND PETIT PALAIS

The Grand and Petit Palais, on avenue Winston Churchill, were built for the World Fair in 1900. The **Grand Palais** ❸ (3 avenue du Général Eisenhower, 8th; www.grandpalais.fr; daily except Tue 10am–8pm, Wed until 10pm; charge), with its 5,000 sq m (54,000 sq ft) of space, hosts blockbuster art exhibitions and the annual Paris Motor Show. There is a cool new restaurant, **Minipalais**, see page 115, which is a good stop for lunch.

The Rococo-style **Petit Palais** ❹ (avenue Winston Churchill, 8th; www.petit-palais.paris.fr; Tue–Sun 10am–6pm, Thu until 8pm for special exhibitions; charge) houses the collection of the **Musée des Beaux-Arts de la Ville de Paris**. The building, inspired by the Grand Trianon at Versailles (see page 92), with its polychrome marble, mag-

The famous Ladurée macaroons

nificent long gallery and arcaded garden, houses the municipal fine and decorative arts collection, including Greek and Roman antiquities, icons, paintings and Art Nouveau furniture.

PALAIS DE LA DÉCOUVERTE

Behind the Grand Palais on avenue Franklin D. Roosevelt is the **Palais de la Découverte ❺** (www.palais-decouverte.fr; Tue–Sat 9.30am–6pm, Sun 10am–7pm; charge), a science museum that is particularly fun for children. It is arranged as a series of interactive experiments, with highlights including a planetarium, electrostatics room and an area explaining acoustics.

PLACE DE LE CONCORDE

Now proceeding to the bottom of the Champs-Élysées, you enter **place de la Concorde ❻**, flanked by copies of Guillaume Coustou's *Marly Horses* (the originals are in the Louvre). In the centre of this grand square is an **obelisk** from the tomb of Ramses III in Luxor. It was a gift from the Viceroy of Egypt in 1829 and took four years to get here. Previously, this spot had been occupied by the guillotine, and it was here that Louis XVI was beheaded in January 1793.

On the west side of the square is the **Jardin des Tuileries** (see page 32), whereas on the north side are two identical palaces, designed in 1753 by Louis

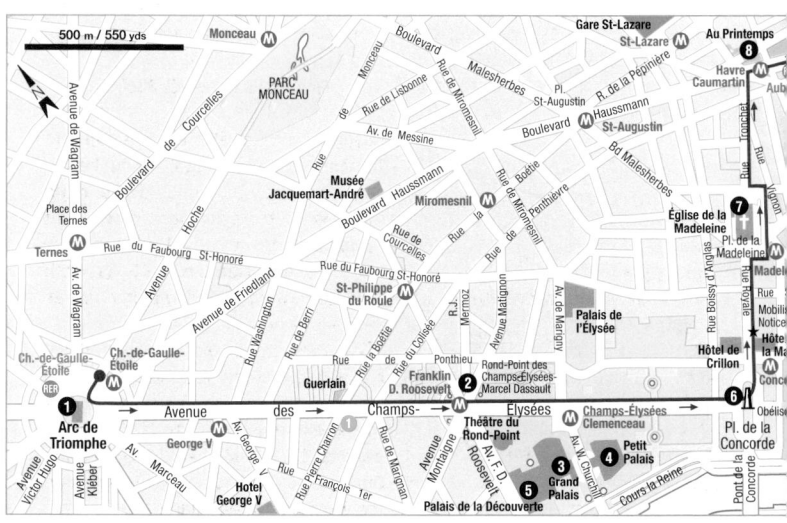

The Madeleine   *Ornate doorway at the Grand Palais*

XV's architect, Ange-Jacques Gabriel. The right-hand one houses the naval ministry; the other is the **Hôtel de Crillon** (closed until 2015 for renovation). The latter was where Marie Antoinette came for piano lessons, where the American delegation to the Paris Peace Conference stayed in 1919, and the German high command ensconced itself in World War II.

Walk up rue Royale between the two palaces. On the wall of no. 4 is an oddity: a mobilisation notice, now framed, from the start of World War I.

THE MADELEINE

Before long, rue Royale opens out into **place de la Madeleine**, dominated by the neoclassical **Église de la Madeleine** ❼ (daily 9.30am–7pm; free). The church is the fruit of 80 years of anguished debate and false starts – the site was mooted for a stock exchange, public ballroom, library and railway station – until 1806, when Napoleon ordered that a temple to his army be built by Barthélemy Vignon. It took until 1842 for it to be finished, by which time it was decided to consecrate it as a church. Today, it is noted for having one of the finest pipe organs in the city. There are free music recitals in the church every Sunday at 4pm.

Outside, the square offers a flower market as well as the main branches of France's best-known delicatessens, **Fauchon** and **Hédiard**, and the showroom of **Maille**, the mustard makers.

GRANDS BOULEVARDS

Beyond the Madeleine, walk up rue Tronchet then turn right on to boulevard Haussmann, home to the city's most famous department stores, **Au Printemps** ❽ at no. 64, and, nearby at no. 40, **Galeries Lafayette** ❾, both as noteworthy for their architecture as their vast stock.

At place Diaghilev turn right down rue Scribe. On this road are the 1862 **Grand Hotel** and the **Musée de la Parfumerie Fragonard** (9 rue Scribe; www.fragonard.com; Mon–Sat 9am–6pm, Sun until 5pm; free), which focuses on the art of perfume-making.

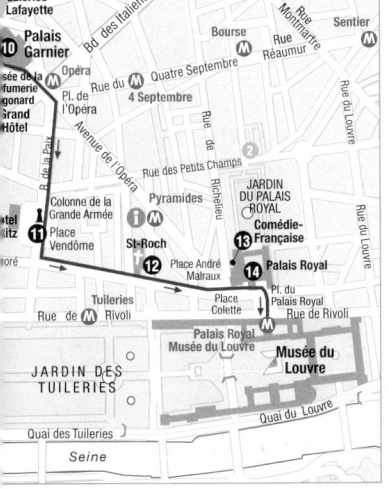

Fashion emporium Galeries Lafayette

OPÉRA

Now turn left on to rue Auber to arrive at place de l'Opéra, where the **Palais Garnier** ⑩ (www.operadeparis.fr; daily 10am–5pm, mid-July–Aug until 6pm; charge) puts on opera and ballet alongside the newer Opéra Bastille (see page 55). It takes its name from its architect, Charles Garnier, who in 1860 was commissioned by Napoleon III to build an opera house reflecting the pomp and opulence of the Second Empire. The auditorium, decked out in velvet and gilt, is dominated by a vast chandelier, which once crashed down on the audience in 1896. The ceiling was painted by Marc Chagall in 1964. A visit also takes in a library and museum, displaying scores, costumes and sets.

PLACE VENDÔME

As you leave place de l'Opéra, take rue de la Paix, which leads southwest at the bottom of the square. Its exclusive jewellers give a hint as to why it is the most expensive street in the French version of the Monopoly board game.

At its end, you reach the elegant **place Vendôme** ⑪. The square's centrepiece was originally an equestrian statue of Louis XIV, erected in 1699. This was destroyed during the Revolution and then replaced by Napoleon with the **Colonne de la Grande Armée**, modelled on Trajan's Column in Rome and made from 1,250 cannons captured from the Austrians and Russians. This in turn was pulled down during the 1871 Commune, only to be rebuilt later.

All the same, the square has in fact survived revolution and insurrection remarkably well. Today it is home to wealthy bankers, the salons of leading dress designers, top-price jewellers and the Hotel Ritz (closed for renovation until late 2014), where Princess Diana spent her last evening before her fateful car journey in 1997.

ST-ROCH

At the southern end of place Vendôme, turn left on to rue St-Honoré. Before long, on your left at no. 296, is the late Baroque church of **St-Roch** ⑫ (daily 8.30am–7pm; free). Begun in the 1650s by architect Jacques Lemercier, who also worked on the Louvre, it contains the funerary monuments of landscape designer André Le Nôtre, the playwright Corneille and encyclopedist Diderot. On the church's exterior are pockmarks from musket shot after Napoleon's troops put down a Royalist revolt here in 1795.

COMÉDIE-FRANÇAISE

Now continue to place André Malraux, home to the French national theatre, the **Comédie-Française** ⑬ (entrance on place Colette; tel: 08 25 10 16 80; www.comedie-francaise.fr). Most productions are of the classical repertoire,

Jewellers line Place Vendôme

Buren's columns at the Palais Royal

by playwrights including Molière, Racine and Corneille.

PALAIS ROYAL

On the far side of the theatre is the **Palais Royal** ⓮. The palace's main courtyard, which is entered through the archway, contains 250 black-and-white striped columns, erected by artist Daniel Buren in 1986. Beyond are elegant gardens (daily dawn–dusk; free) enclosed by a three-storey peristyle erected in 1780 to house cafés, shops and apartments, and, with its rents, to replenish the coffers of its owners, the Orléans family, after a century of profligate spending. The passageways are enjoying a regeneration sparked by the opening of fashion designer Marc Jacobs' flagship store here.

Built for Cardinal Richelieu, and subsequently the childhood home of Louis XIV, the palace passed into the hands of the dukes of Orléans in the early 1700s. They turned it into a den of gambling and prostitution and forbade the police entrance. It was a focal point for intrigue during the Revolution, and afterwards, once restored to the Orléans, as iniquitous as before. Wellington supposedly lost so much money in its casinos that Parisians claimed they had recouped the cost of their war reparations. Today, it is a tamer place, housing the Ministry of Culture and Constitutional Council.

Slip out of the northern end of the Palais Royal's gardens and cross the tiny rue des Petits-Champs. To your left are **Galerie Vivienne** and **Galerie Colbert**, beautifully preserved skylit passages with mosaic floors and brass lamps, and both lined with shops.

At this, the route's end, you can rejoin the metro just south of the Palais Royal or, to the north, visit **Willi's Wine Bar**, see ❷, for a drink.

Food and Drink

❶ LADURÉE

75 Champs-Élysées, 8th; tel: 01 40 75 08 75; Mon–Thu 7.30am–11.30pm, Fri until 12.30am, Sat 8.30am–12.30am, Sun until 11.30pm; €€–€€€
This Parisian 'laboratory' of master macaroon-makers produces tiptop macaroons every day and develops new flavours such as rose petal or liquorice. At this Champs-Élysées branch you can also enjoy breakfast or a full meal of French classics at the restaurant amid Louis XIV-style decor. Other branches include 16 rue Royale (also on this walk).

❷ WILLI'S WINE BAR

13 rue des Petits Champs, 1st; tel: 01 42 61 05 09; closed Sun; €€€
As well as dozens of wines from around the world sold by the glass or bottle, this bar serves a variety of traditional, seasonal French dishes along with simpler offerings such as *croques* and platters of charcuterie.

Centre Pompidou's 'inside-out' architecture

BEAUBOURG AND LES HALLES

This compact area is really in the thick of things, historically, artistically and commercially. Whereas once the city's food markets drew the crowds, today, the attractions are modern art, historic monuments and upmarket food shops.

DISTANCE: 2.5km (1.5 miles)
TIME: Half a day
START: Centre Pompidou
END: Rue de Rivoli
POINTS TO NOTE: Allow at least a couple of hours in the Centre Pompidou – longer, if you are particularly keen on modern and contemporary art.

This route starts at the front of the Centre Pompidou, where the sloping cobbled terrace acts as a stage for fire-eaters, mime artists, hair-braiders and musicians.

CENTRE POMPIDOU

The **Centre Pompidou** ❶ (place Georges Pompidou; www.centrepompidou. fr; Wed–Mon 11am–10pm; tickets until 8pm; charge except for under 18s), or 'Beaubourg,' as it is known locally, after the street that runs behind it, continues where the Musée d'Orsay (see page 39) leaves off, with art from 1905 onwards.

The architecture

The building was completed in 1977 to designs by architects Renzo Piano and Richard Rogers. The museum is now so popular that it is hard to appreciate the initial storm of criticism regarding its 'inside-out' architecture (blue units transport air conditioning, green ones are water circulation, red tubes are transport routes and yellow ones indicate electric circuits).

Entrance and services

Inside, on the ground floor, there is a complete posting of the centre's events and exhibits. There is often a free exhibition in the massive entrance hall itself, while on the mezzanine level there is a post office, internet café and a shop selling a selection of works by modern designers. On the first floor there is a public library and a cinema.

The permanent collection

A selection from the permanent art collection of 60,000 works is on levels 4 and 5. Parts are rehung every year. The period from 1905 to the 1960s

The colourful Stravinsky Fountain

is dealt with on level 5, with works by artists such as Kandinsky, Klee, Klein, Matisse, Picasso and Pollock, and sections on Dadaism and Surrealism. Art from the 1960s to the present day is on level 4 and includes works by Andy Warhol, Verner Panton, Joseph Beuys, Jean Dubuffet and Anselm Kiefer.

Studio Brancusi, IRCAM and Stravinsky Fountain

In front of the Pompidou is a pavilion containing the studio (Wed–Mon 2–6pm; included in main ticket) of Romanian-born sculptor, Constantin Brancusi (1876–1957). The artist lived in this studio for 30 years, bequeathing it to the French state on his death. It has been set up here just as he left it.

Next to the Pompidou, and part of the same organisation, is the Institute of Research and Co-ordination into Acoustics and Music (IRCAM), on place Igor Stravinsky. This centre, created by composer Pierre Boulez, hosts concerts of avant-garde music.

Between the Centre Pompidou and the church of St-Merri is the **Stravinsky Fountain**, created by artists Niki de Saint-Phalle and Jean Tinguely as a homage to composer Igor Stravinsky's *Firebird* ballet. Forms and figures represent the story and spout water. The square is a favourite summer picnic spot but crowded with pigeons.

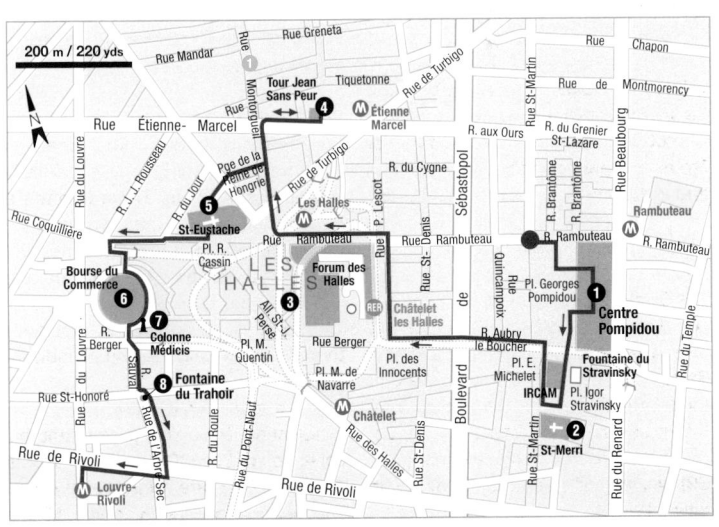

A rue Montorgueil culinary institution

ST-MERRI

Beyond the Stravinsky Fountain, on the south side of the square is the Gothic church of **St-Merri** ❷ (76 rue de la Verrerie; www.saintmerri.org; Mon–Sat 3–7pm; free). It dates mostly from the 16th century, but its bell has been tolling since 1331, which makes it the oldest in Paris. There are music recitals at 8pm on Saturdays and 4pm on Sundays.

RED LIGHTS

Exiting the church on rue St-Martin, turn right, up towards the Pompidou, and then left at rue Aubry le Boucher. Go straight on, across the busy boulevard de Sébastopol and on to rue Berger. At the corner of rue St-Denis, take a good look up and down. Rue St-Denis is the city's main red-light district. The area in which you stand is fairly tame, though things become more overt further along.

LES HALLES

Rue Berger now opens out into place Joachim du Bellay. The Fontaine des Innocents, the Renaissance fountain in the middle, was moved here from the nearby Cimetière des Innocents, which was demolished in 1786.

Leaving the place by rue Pierre Lescot on your right, you come to **Les Halles** ❸. The name refers to the covered food market that was established

here by King Philippe Auguste in 1183. In the 1850s, huge glass-and-iron buildings were erected, and Emile Zola later wrote a novel, *The Belly of Paris* (1873), set around the area. Sadly, in 1971 the structure was demolished in the interests of safety and urban renewal, and the markets moved to the southern suburb of Rungis. Today, the site is occupied by a widely disliked multi-level shopping centre, although regeneration on and around the complex has started.

TOUR JEAN SANS PEUR

Past Les Halles, turn left on to rue Rambuteau and right on to rue Montorgueil. Where rue Étienne-Marcel, now one of the city's most fashionable shopping streets, crosses rue Montorgueil, turn right for the **Tour Jean Sans Peur** ❹ (20 rue Étienne-Marcel; www.tourjean sanspeur.com; mid-Apr–mid-Nov Wed–Sun 1.30–6pm, mid-Nov–mid Apr Wed, Sat–Sun 1.30–6pm; charge), a fortified town house built 1409–11 by Jean, Duke of Burgundy.

The duke acquired his nickname, meaning 'John the Fearless', from military exploits in Bulgaria against the Turks. On return to Paris, he assassinated his rival, Louis d'Orléans, and sparked the Hundred Years' War between the Armagnac and Burgundian factions. Jean fled, but returned two years later and, necessarily security conscious, added the tower.

'Écoute' sculpture outside St-Eustache

ST-EUSTACHE

Retracing your way back down rue Montorgueil, perhaps stopping en route at **Stohrer**, see ❶, take the narrow passage de la Reine de Hongrie on your right, then continue over to the Impasse St-Eustache, which leads to the church of **St-Eustache** ❺ (2 impasse St-Eustache; Mon–Fri 9.30am–7pm, Sat–Sun 9am–7pm; free). Built from 1532 to 1640, it has a Gothic exterior and fine Renaissance interior. Its 8,000-pipe organ is highly renowned: Berlioz and Liszt played here in the 19th century, and recitals are still held weekly, at 5.30pm on Sundays.

Around Place René-Cassin

Emerging from the other (south) side of the church, you find yourself on place René-Cassin with its massive sculpture by Henri de Miller of a giant head and cupped hand, entitled *Écoute* (Listen). Continue west on rue Coquillière. A curiosity on your right is **E. Dehillerin**, purveyors of pots and pans to Paris's chefs.

BOURSE DE COMMERCE

The rotunda on your left is the **Bourse de Commerce** ❻ (2 rue de Viarmes; Mon–Fri 9am–6pm; free access to main hall). The Bourse was built in 1767 on the site of Marie de Médicis' palace, and functioned as the city's grain market. Today, it houses the Chamber of Commerce.

ASTROLOGER'S COLUMN

As you leave the Bourse, turn left and go round the back to find the **Colonne Médicis** ❼. The plaque at its base states that the pillar is the sole relic of the manor house constructed in 1572 by Catherine de Médicis (wife of Henri II). She had a 31m (102ft) -high tower built for her astrologer, Cosimo Ruggieri, who, with his patron, regularly climbed up the spiral staircase within to read the future in the stars. Unfortunately, visitors can no longer go inside.

FONTAINE DU TRAHOIR

Head down rue Sauval, turn left at rue St-Honoré and then immediately right on to rue de l'Arbre-Sec. At no. 52 is La Galcante, a library selling historic newspapers and other printed ephemera. On the street corner is the **Fontaine du Trahoir** ❽, a fountain rebuilt by Soufflot in 1776 and dripping with stone icicles. Follow the road to rue de Rivoli and turn right to rejoin the metro at Louvre-Rivoli.

Food and Drink

❶ STOHRER

51 rue Montorgueil, 2nd; tel: 01 42 33 38 20; €

Founded in 1730, this pâtisserie is where the *baba au rhum* was invented. Also serves savoury snacks.

Through to Place des Vosges

MARAIS AND BASTILLE

Among the most vibrant areas of town, the Marais and the Bastille are an unlikely but successful blend of ingredients: aristocratic mansions, the centre of the gay scene, the home of the Jewish community, and a throbbing nightlife.

DISTANCE: 4.5km (2.75 miles)
TIME: A full day
START: Hôtel de Ville
END: Place de la Bastille
POINTS TO NOTE: It is not intended that you visit every museum.
There is, however, the opportunity to combine a stroll in the historic streets with some shopping, lunch, a museum tour and finally a rest in a park or café.

The area covered in the first part of this tour was once a swamp – 'marais' is French for 'marsh'. It was drained in the 16th century and developed as an aristocratic residential district, until, with the rise of Versailles, it fell into neglect. Largely untouched by town planner Baron Haussmann in the 19th century, it fell into further decline, until by the 1960s it was derelict and rat infested. Due to be cleared, it was saved by Culture Minister André Malraux, who safeguarded many of the buildings and initiated the restoration. Today it is a fashionable quarter home to a mix of grandiose and small-scale buildings, quaint boutiques, cosy cafés, hip bars and bistros.

HÔTEL DE VILLE

Begin at the **Hôtel de Ville** ❶ (29 rue de Rivoli; www.paris.fr; Mon–Sat 10am–7pm), since 1357 the seat of local government in Paris. The building is a recreation of the original structure, commissioned by François I in 1533 and gutted by fire during the Paris Commune of 1871.

It has been the scene of many historical events, including the proclamation of the Third Republic in 1870 and Charles de Gaulle's famous speech to the assembled crowds on 25 August 1944 during the Liberation of Paris.

Its most notable features are the extravagant Salle des Fêtes (ballroom), a magnificent staircase and some opulent chandeliers. On the north side, on rue de Rivoli, is an entrance to an exhibition with information about the city.

Place de la Bastille and the Colonne de Juillet

THE MARAIS

Head north from the pedestrianised square in front of the Hôtel de Ville, where, in medieval times, hangings and other gruesome executions took place. Cross the rue de Rivoli, walk up rue du Temple and turn right at rue Ste-Croix-de-la-Bretonnerie, the centre of the gay scene. Turn left off this road on to rue des Archives and then continue until you reach rue des Francs-Bourgeois.

Hôtel de Soubise and Hôtel de Rohan

At no. 60, in the **Hôtel de Soubise** ❷, is one of three sites in France housing the French National Archives (Mon, Wed–Fri 10am–5.30pm, Sat–Sun 2–5.30pm; charge), opened by Napoleon in 1808 and containing documents from the Merovingians to the Ancien Régime. Around the corner at 87 rue Vieille-du-Temple is the **Hôtel de Rohan** ❸, which hosts exhibitions relating to French history.

If for nothing else, it is worth a visit for the magnificent buildings themselves, which were home to the Guise family from 1553; it is probably from here that the Catholic League planned the St Bartholemew's Day Massacre. In 1700, the Duke de Rohan, Prince of Soubise, bought the estate and revamped it, with Rococo interiors decorated by Boucher, Lemoine and van Loo. The gardens are quite lovely too.

Lunch options and shopping

While on rue Vieille du Temple, there are several good options for lunch, including **Le Petit Fer à Cheval**, see ❶. Back on rue des Francs-Bourgeois there are designer boutiques and cafés, too. The Marais is one of the few Paris districts in which a large number of shops open for business on a Sunday, its busiest and most crowded day of the week.

When sated, continue a little further to find rue Elzévir on your left.

Musée Cognacq-Jay

The outside of the 1580s mansion at no. 8 rue Elzévir is understated, but inside is the exquisite fine and decorative art collection of Ernest Cognacq, who founded La Samaritaine department store in 1870, and his wife Marie-Louise Jay, in the **Musée Cognacq-Jay** ❹ (www.cognac-jay.paris.fr; Tue–Sun 10am–6pm; free).

Here, 18th-century refinement is embodied in salons and 'cabinets' with the feel of a private house. On the panelled walls are paintings and drawings by Chardin, Nattier, Fragonard, Watteau, Reynolds, Guardi and Canaletto. Displayed on delicate furniture and in cabinets are Meissen porcelain figures by master modeller J.J. Kändler.

Musée National Picasso

On nearby rue de Thorigny is the **Musée National Picasso** (5 rue de Thorigny,

Musée Carnavalet china

www.musee-picasso.fr; closed for renovation until late 2013). The museum is housed in the Hôtel Salé, so-called because its 17thcentury owner grew rich through collecting taxes on salt. The paintings and other works of art in the collection were given to the state on the artist's death. Not all are by Picasso: his personal collection includes works by Cézanne, Matisse (his great rival), Modigliani and Braque.

Hôtel Carnavalet

For now, though, the next stop is the **Musée de l'Histoire de Paris** ❺ (Hôtel Carnavalet, 23 rue de Sévigné; www.carn avalet.paris.fr; Tue–Sun 10am–6pm; free). This is the city's historical museum, set within two adjoining 16th- to 17th-century mansions. In over 100 rooms, it tells the story of Paris from Roman times to the present using paintings, memorabilia and historic interiors.

The museum dates from 1866, when Baron Haussmann convinced the city to purchase many of the fine interiors of the aristocratic mansions he was then demolishing to make way for the new boulevards. These interiors were moved to the Carnavalet, one of Paris's first Renaissance buildings, and, fittingly, home from 1677 to 1696 to

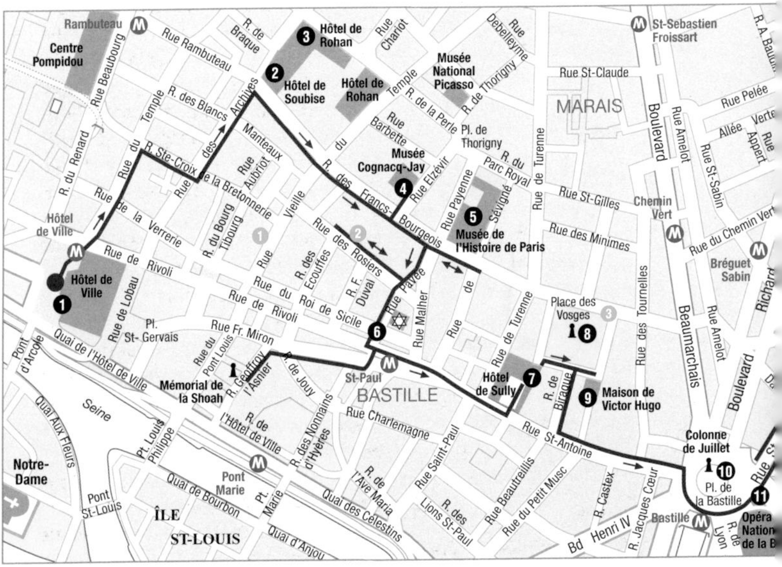

Carnavalet painting　　　　　　　　　　　　　　　*The Jewish Quarter*

Madame de Sévigné, whose writings reveal so much about 17th-century aristocratic life.

Among the exhibits are the spinning wheel used by Marie Antoinette when in prison, as well as her son's tin soldiers (rooms 105–106); the chains used on one of the last prisoners at the Bastille (room 102); paintings of the prostitutes working the galleries of the Palais Royal (room 117); the Art Nouveau interiors of the Salon du Café de Paris and a jewellery shop from rue Royale (rooms 141 and 142); and Proust's cork-lined bedroom, in which he wrote much of his seven-volume masterpiece *À la recherche du temps perdu* (room 147).

Jewish Quarter

Leaving the Carnavalet, take rue Pavée opposite to reach the Jewish Quarter also known as 'Pletzl', which is Yiddish for 'little place'. Off to the right on rue des Rosiers are several Jewish bakeries and restaurants, including the excellent **L'As du Fallafel**, see , a by-product, like many, of the Sephardic immigration after the French withdrawal from North Africa.

At 10 rue Pavée is the extraordinary **Synagogue** ❻ (tel: 01 48 87 21 54; visits by request only; free). It is architecturally notable for its 1913 Art Nouveau facade by Hector Guimard, who also designed the furnishings inside. The building was severely damaged by a bomb (along with six other Parisian synagogues) during anti-Semitic demonstrations on the evening of Yom Kippur 1941. It was restored and is now a national monument. A few minutes' walk west of here is the **Mémorial de la Shoah** (17 rue Geoffroy l'Asnier, 4th; www.memorialdelashoah.org; Mon–Wed, Fri, Sun 10am–6pm, Thu until 10pm, closed Jewish holidays; free) which is the most important centre in Europe devoted to the Holocaust and has a permanent exhibition on the concentration camps.

Retrace your steps and continue along rue Pavée and turn left on to rue de Rivoli, which soon becomes rue St-Antoine.

The delightful Place des Vosges

Hôtel de Sully

At no. 62, enter the large wooden doors of the **Hôtel de Sully** ❼ (www.monuments-nationaux.fr; courtyards open daily 9am–7pm). This impressive 17th-century mansion, built to plans by architect Jean Androuet du Cerceau in 1625 and then bought in 1635 by Sully (Finance Minister under Henri IV), is the HQ of Monuments Nationaux, the organisation that looks after France's most important historical buildings.

Walk through the cobbled courtyard, and on into the pristine gardens.

Place des Vosges

A gate in the far corner provides an escape on to **place des Vosges** ❽. Built from 1605 to 1612 by Henri IV, this large, elegant square was originally called place Royale, but was renamed in tribute to the first French *département* (county) to pay its war taxes to the Republican government. Famous past residents have included Madame de Sévigné, salon hostess and letter writer, at no. 1bis (born here in 1626), poet Théophile Gautier and writer Alphonse Daudet at no. 8, and Cardinal Richelieu at no. 21. Upmarket pâtissier Carette, see ❸, has a tea room here which is a good spot for a pit stop.

Maison de Victor Hugo

Located in the southeast corner of the square, at no. 6, is the **Maison de Victor Hugo** ❾ (www.paris.fr; Tue–Sun 10am–6pm; free), erstwhile home of the author of *Les Misérables* and *The Hunchback of Notre-Dame*. Hugo lived here from 1832 to 1848, until Napoleon III's coup d'état forced him, as a staunch republican, into 20 years of exile on Guernsey. Inside, you can see his rooms, some furnished with a few of his own pieces – he was an expert, though eccentric, carpenter – as well as a number of his drawings and first editions.

BASTILLE

Leaving place des Vosges and the Marais behind, walk down rue de Birague and turn left at rue St-Antoine. A sign of how things have changed around Bastille is to be found at 17 rue de la Roquette, just off rue St-Sabin. The bar La Rotonde now attracts the young and hip, but was previously a brotherl whose owner was shot dead by a blind accordion player.

Place de la Bastille

The vast **place de la Bastille** ❿ takes its name from the notorious prison stormed by revolutionaries on 14 July 1789. On its capture, only seven prisoners remained inside, but the rebels found a useful supply of arms and gunpowder. The Banque de France office now stands on its site.

In the centre of the square is the **Colonne de Juillet** (July Column), which was erected in the 19th century to honour victims of the 1830 and 1848 rev-

Suitably elegant buskers in the Marais

olutions. The golden statue at the top, the *Génie de la Bastille*, is a representation of Liberty.

Opéra National de la Bastille

On the southeast side is the **Opéra National de la Bastille** ⓫ (120 rue de Lyon; www.operadeparis.fr; charge for tours, cash only). One of Mitterrand's *grands projets* (see page 30), it was constructed in 1989 to designs by Canadian-based Uruguayan Carlos Ott, but has since been plagued with criticism: for its acoustics, its vast cost and the poor quality of its architecture. Netting has already been put up to stop its granite slabs falling down.

The fashionable east

If you take rue de la Roquette off place de la Bastille and turn right on to rue de Lappe, you find yourself on a street lined with bars, nightclubs, cafés and boutiques, a reflection of the area's fashionable status, which boomed in the 1990s. (Nowadays, it's still trendy, although not quite as cutting edge as it once was). The area's fashion credentials are also reflected in its peppering with contemporary galleries. At the end of rue de Lappe, turn left on to rue de Charonne, where **Lavignes Bastille** ⓬ (est.1973), at no. 27, is one of the best-known galleries in the neighbourhood (Andy Warhol exhibited here).

For more contemporary art, additional galleries can be found further up on your left on rue Keller. To return to Bastille, retrace your steps or turn left at the northern end of rue Keller on to rue de la Roquette.

Food and Drink

① LE PETIT FER À CHEVAL

30 rue Vieille du Temple, 4th; tel: 01 42 72 47 47; daily till 2am; €€
Cramped but fun café-bistro with a horseshoe-shaped bar out front and small box of a dining room with old metro benches at the back. A case study in artful insouciance.

② L'AS DU FALLAFEL

34 rue des Rosiers, 4th; tel: 01 48 87 63 60; closed Fri dinner and Sat; €

The place for fallafel. Try the special (vegetarian) sandwich: garlicky chickpea balls, hummous, fried aubergine, red cabbage, salted cucumber and harissa. Lamb chawarmas are also recommended. Hectic but fun ambience. Takeaway also available.

③ CARETTE

25 place des Vosges, 4th; tel: 01 48 87 94 07; daily 8am–11.30pm; credit cards over €15; €
Smart tearoom for light savoury snacks and mouth-watering cakes and desserts.

English bookshop Shakespeare & Co

THE LATIN QUARTER

This university area takes you from Roman remains to medieval theological colleges, to Enlightenment seats of learning, to the student riots of 1968. And the tradition continues today, with students and academics smoking outside the libraries, drinking in the cafés and browsing in the bookshops.

> **DISTANCE:** 3km (2 miles)
> **TIME:** A full day
> **START:** Jardin des Plantes
> **END:** Place St-Michel
> **POINT TO NOTE:** The first part of the route is good for children, who will love the Jardin des Plantes.

The route begins across the road from the Gare d'Austerlitz, on place Valhubert, at the entrance to the **Jardin des Plantes** ❶ (Botanical Gardens; daily 7.30am–8pm, until 5.30pm in winter; free).

JARDIN DES PLANTES

The gardens were established by Louis XIII's physician in 1626 as a source of medicinal herbs and opened to the public in 1640 as the 'Jardin du Roi'. In the 1700s, a maze, amphitheatre and several museums were added.

On your left as you enter is the first of these museums, that of palaeontology and comparative anatomy, the **Galerie de Paléontologie et d'Anatomie com-parée** (daily 10am–5pm; charge), displaying fossils, skeletons and shells. Outside are huge replica dinosaurs.

Museum of Mineralogy and Geology

Now make your way to the statue of the zoologist Jean-Baptiste Lamarck, and from here walk up the avenue of plane trees to the statue of an illustrious former keeper of the gardens, Georges-Louis Leclerc, Count de Buffon. En route, you pass the rose garden in front of the newly renovated **Galerie de Minéralogie et de Géologie** (Museum of Mineralogy and Geology; daily 10am–6pm; charge), which contains meteorites, minerals, jewels and giant crystals.

The Zoo

On the opposite side, is the **Ménagerie** (daily 9am–6pm; charge). This zoo was established during the Revolution with animals from royal and aristocratic collections.

Beyond the statue of de Buffon is the **Grande Galerie de l'Évolution** (Wed–Mon 10am–6pm; charge), opened in 1889 to display part of the collection

The mosque's tranquil courtyard

of 7 million skeletons, insects, and stuffed birds and mammals. Most are now in an underground research centre, but following renovation, the exhibition space shows some 7,000 choice specimens, including 257 endangered or extinct species.

MOSQUÉE DE PARIS

Leaving the gardens by the gate on rue Geoffroy St-Hilaire, cross over towards the corner of rue Daubenton and the **Mosquée de Paris** ❷ (Paris Mosque; 2bis place du Puits de l'Ermite; tours daily 9am–noon and 2–6pm; charge). This Hispano-Moorish-style complex was built in 1922 to commemorate North African participation in World War I. It incorporates a museum of Muslim art, a Moroccan-style market, a pretty tearoom, see ❶, and a Turkish bath.

ARÈNES DE LUTÈCE

Turn left out of the tearoom and continue walking north along rue Geoffroy St-Hilaire. Go straight on at the crossroads, as the road becomes rue Linné. Take a left into rue Arènes. On your right is the entrance to the **Arènes de Lutèce** ❸ (daily 8am–5.30pm, till 9.30pm in summer; free). This Roman amphitheatre was rediscovered in the 1860s during the construction of the nearby rue Monge. Where gladiators once fought

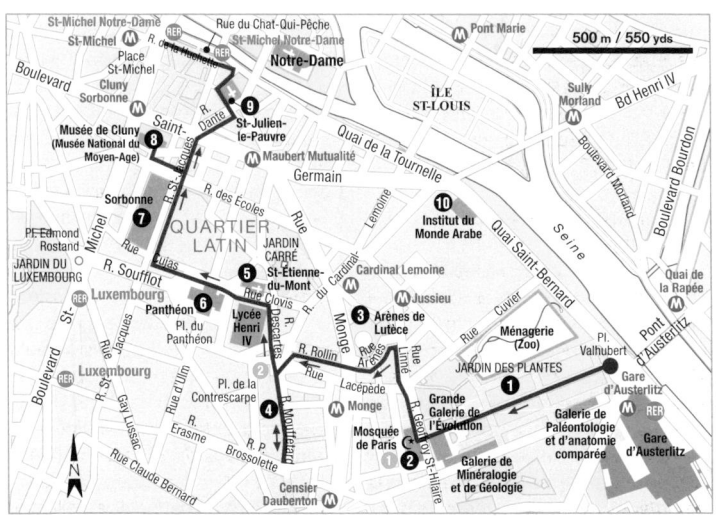

Panthéon fresco

before an audience of 15,000, elderly men now play boules.

RUE MOUFFETARD

As you leave, turn right and climb the few steps to rue Rollin. At the end of this road, turn left on to rue du Cardinal-Lemoine. You soon come to **place de la Contrescarpe**, with its pleasant Café Delmas, see ②.

On the far side of the square is **rue Mouffetard ④**, a former Roman road, famous for its food market (Tue–Sat, all day, and Sun am).

TOWARDS THE PANTHÉON

Retrace your steps to place de la Contrescarpe, then keep going, along rue Descartes, into the heart of the Latin Quarter. This university area derives

its name from the fact that Latin was widely spoken here in the Middle Ages. Turn left at rue Clovis, to see, on your left, the **Lycée Henri IV**, one of France's most elite secondary schools, and, on your right, the church of **St-Étienne-du-Mont ⑤** (place Ste-Geneviève; Tue–Fri 8.45am–7.45pm, Sat–Sun 8.45am–noon and 2–7.45pm; free). The scientist and philosopher Blaise Pascal is buried here along with St Geneviève, the patron saint of Paris.

The Panthéon

Coming out into the vast place du Panthéon, the neoclassical **Panthéon ⑥** (www.pantheonparis.com; daily 10am–6pm; charge) looms before you. It was designed by Soufflot as a church to St Geneviève for Louis XV, who wanted to give thanks for his recovery from illness. After the Revolution it became a Temple to Reason and the burial place of the nation's great minds, including Voltaire, Rousseau, Hugo, Zola, and Pierre and Marie Curie. Another highlight is a 67m (220ft) replica of Foucault's pendulum (an experiment to show the rotation of the earth).

THE SORBONNE

Next take rue Cujas off the square to your right, turn right on to rue St-Jacques and head down the hill. The **Sorbonne ⑦**, one of the oldest colleges (1253) of the university of Paris, is on your left. The buildings date mainly from the

---

Medieval tapestry

The Musée de Cluny's tapestry series *The Lady and the Unicorn* is one of the greatest works of art of the Middle Ages in Europe. It depicts the five senses plus a sixth, mysterious, sense. In this last scene, the lady puts into her jewel-case the collar that she was wearing in the other five. Above her is the inscription, 'To My Only Desire'. The most popular theory is that this signifies the refusal of temptation, and the renunciation of the five senses, previously sated.

Cluny's 'The Lady and the Unicorn'

late 19th century, although the domed chapel, in which Cardinal Richelieu is buried, is 17th century. At the bottom of the hill on your right is the Collège de France, founded in 1530 as a humanist alternative to the decidedly Catholic Sorbonne.

MUSÉE DE CLUNY

Turn left on to rue des Écoles then right at the square Painlevé for the **Musée de Cluny – Musée National du Moyen-Âge** ❽ (Wed–Mon 9.15am–5.45pm; charge). Once the residence of the Abbots of Cluny, this is the only surviving Gothic residence in Paris. It also incorporates the remains of a huge Gallo-Roman bathhouse complex, built c.200 AD.

On display in the main museum are medieval manuscripts, textiles (notably the *Lady and the Unicorn* tapestries – see box), stained glass and sculpture, including those crafted in 1220 for the front of Notre-Dame (see page 26).

TOWARDS THE SEINE

After the museum, return to rue St-Jacques and continue downhill, bearing right on to rue Dante.

Square Viviani
A little further on is **square Viviani**, on the far side of which is the 12th-century church of **St-Julien-le-Pauvre** ❾, originally a sanctuary for pilgrims on their way to Compostella.

Taking rue St-Julien towards the river you reach quirky English-language bookshop **Shakespeare & Co.** (Mon–Fri 10am–11pm, Sat–Sun 11am–11pm). On the pavement by the river are *bouquinistes* (riverside bookstalls) and if you look east, you'll see the striking **Institut du Monde Arabe** ❿ (1 rue des Fossés-St-Bernard, 5th; closed Mon). Designed by Jean Nouvel, it houses a cultural centre. Views from the rooftop restaurant are stunning.

Rue de la Huchette
Walking west, cross rue St-Jacques and go down **rue de la Huchette**. Look out for **rue du Chat-Qui-Pêche**, the city's narrowest street. on the right. You emerge on place St-Michel.

Food and Drink

❶ MOSQUÉE DE PARIS TEAROOM
39 rue Geoffroy-St-Hilaire, 5th; tel: 01 43 31 38 20; open daily; €
This beautiful Moorish tearoom with a tiled interior and shady terrace.

❷ CAFÉ DELMAS
2 place de la Contrescarpe, 5th; tel: 01 43 26 51 26; daily 7.30am–2am; €€
You don't really come here for the food (although the burgers, bagels and hotdogs are decent enough) but to sit on the terrace to look out onto one of the prettiest squares in Paris.

Legendary Left Bank Café de Flore

ST-GERMAIN

With its elegant streets and squares, St-Germain is a magnet for designer fashion shops, chic cafés and restaurants. But before the glossy present was a more rumbustious past: revolutionaries plotted, actors drank, and Hemingway stole pigeons from the Jardin du Luxembourg to cook and eat.

> **DISTANCE:** 3km (2 miles)
> **TIME:** A full day
> **START:** Place St-Michel
> **END:** Jardin du Luxembourg
> **POINTS TO NOTE:** End your walk with a picnic in the Jardin du Luxembourg.

The route begins at **place St-Michel ❶**, with its fountain of St Michael slaying a dragon. Head west on to rue St-André-des-Arts, into a warren of streets full of shops, bars and restaurants. Turn left on to rue de l'Éperon, right on to rue du Jardinet, then continue to cour de Rohan.

HISTORIC QUARTER

You finally emerge on to the **cour du Commerce St-André ❷**, where you should turn left. During the Revolution, Danton lived at no. 1 on this cobbled passage and, in the courtyard of no. 9, Dr Guillotin was testing his gruesome invention on sheep.

Le Procope

On a tiny road parallel, look out for **Le Procope** (13 rue de l'Ancienne-Comédie; Sun–Wed 11.30am–midnight, Thu–Sat until 1am), supposedly the oldest surviving café in Paris. It started as a coffee house in 1686, and playwrights Racine and Molière were reportedly regular customers.

BOULEVARD ST-GERMAIN

Exiting the passage, turn right on to boulevard St-Germain. You soon come to place St-Germain-des-Prés, where one of the city's oldest churches is situated, as well as two famous café-restaurants: the **Café de Flore**, see ❶, and **Les Deux Magots**, see ❷.

St-Germain-des-Prés

The church of **St-Germain-des-Prés ❸** (daily 9am–7pm; free) takes its name from an 8th-century cardinal of Paris, who was buried in the 6th-century abbey of Ste-Croix-St-Vincent on this site.

The present church was built in the 11th and 12th centuries and was once

St-Germain chapel

part of a vast monastery, suppressed during the Revolution. The church survived and is the only Romanesque one left in Paris. In the 19th century it was converted into a saltpetre factory and then underwent several less-than-sensitive restorations. Inside, the 17th-century philosopher René Descartes' ashes are interred under the window in the second chapel.

Outside, in square Laurent-Prache, are relics of a magnificent chapel built in 1255. Look out for Pablo Picasso's portrait bust of the poet Guillaume Apollinaire (1880–1918).

From the square, turn right on rue de l'Abbaye, then left on to the pretty rue de Furstemberg.

MUSÉE DELACROIX

The **Musée National Eugène Delacroix** ❹ (www.musee-delacroix.fr; Wed–Mon 9.30am–5pm; charge), at nearby 6 place Furstemberg, comprises the 19th-century painter's former home, studio and garden. The artist moved here in 1857 to be near St-Sulpice, where he had been commissioned to paint several murals. He died in the bedroom in 1863. While the Louvre and Musée d'Orsay house his major Romantic paintings, here you can see smaller works and sketches.

TOWARDS ST-SULPICE

Back on rue de Furstemberg, continue as far as rue Jacob and turn left. At no. 56, peace documents recognising the independence of the US were signed by Benjamin

Detail from St-Sulpice

Franklin and David Hartley, King George III's representative in France.

Retracing your steps, now turn left (north) on rue Bonaparte. On your right by the river is the **Institut de France**. The building houses the Académie Française, whose membership of 40 'immortels' are responsible for the official dictionary of the French language. Back on rue Bonaparte, walk all the way down (south) past a succession of stylish shops. Eventually, you arrive at place St-Sulpice and its lion-flanked Fontaine des Quatre-Évêques. This chic square is used every summer for an antiques fair and poetry fair.

ST-SULPICE

The eastern side of place St-Sulpice is dominated by the vast Italianate church of **St-Sulpice** ❺ (www.paroisse-saint-sulpice-paris.org; daily 7.30am–7.30pm; free). Begun in 1646 to a design by Jean-Baptiste Servandoni, the church took a further five architects and 120 years to complete. The result is ponderous: the towers, one of which is higher than the other (unfinished), have been likened to 'municipal inkwells'. The church has many historical links, though: the Marquis de Sade was baptised here, Victor Hugo was married here, and it featured in Prévost's 18th-century novel *Manon Lescaut*.

Highlights

Inside, the first chapel on the right (Chapelle de Sainte Agnès) was deco-rated by Eugène Delacroix. In the nave are two great conch shells presented to François I by the Republic of Venice. Note also the fine organ with 6,700 pipes and check the noticeboard for details of concerts held in the church.

In the left wing of the transept is a gno-mon, a white marble obelisk with a line of copper leading away from it in the floor, representing the Paris meridian. When the sun shines through the 'eye', located 25m (82ft) above the ground in a tran-sept window facing south, the device is

Montparnasse

On the south side of the Jardin du Lux-embourg is boulevard de Montpar-nasse. In the early 20th century, the area became a magnet for artists, composers and revolutionaries including Chagall, Picasso, Stravinsky and Lenin who gath-ered in cafes and brasseries such as Le Select (No. 99), La Coupole (No. 102), La Rotonde (No. 106) and Le Dôme (No. 108). After World War II, writers and phi-losophers including Jean-Paul Sartre and Simone de Beauvoir moved in, patronis-ing the same places. You can find out about the area's heritage in the Musée du Montparnasse (21 avenue de Maine; Tue–Sun 12.30–7pm; charge). Today the area is best known for its 59-storey skyscraper (www.tourmontparnasse56. com; charge) which has viewing plat-forms, a café and a gourmet restaurant, Le Ciel de Paris, on the 56th floor.

Designer wares, St-Germain

The Luxembourg is the quintessential Paris park

meant to indicate the 'true' midday hour and the approximate date.

ODÉON

Leaving the church, walk along rue St-Sulpice and turn left at rue de Condé to reach **carrefour de l'Odéon**. Next turn right up rue de l'Odéon, an enclave for publishers and antiquarian book-shops for at least 150 years. At no. 12 Sylvia Beach and the original Shake-speare & Co. bookshop (see page 59) first published James Joyce's *Ulysses*.

At the top of the road is the grand neoclassical **Théâtre de l'Odéon 6**, built from 1779 to 1782. It was here that Beaumarchais's *Marriage of Figaro* was first performed in 1784.

Beyond the theatre is rue de Vaugirard, where a pit stop at the engaging **Au Petit Suisse**, see 3, may well be required, before finishing the route in the Jardin du Luxembourg.

JARDIN DU LUXEMBOURG

At the entrance to the **Jardin du Luxembourg 7** (daily dawn–dusk; free) is the **Palais du Luxembourg**, built in the 1620s for Marie de Médicis, widow of Henri IV, by Salomon de Brosse. Its Italianate style was supposed to remind Marie of the Pitti Palace in her native Florence. It now houses the Senate. Next door, at 19 rue de Vaugirard, is the **Musée National du Luxembourg 8** (www.museeduluxembourg.fr; Mon, Fri 10am–10pm, Tue–Thu, Sat–Sun until 7.30pm; charge), France's oldest public art gallery (1750).

Inside the gardens are statues, foun-tains, a boating lake, cafés, a band-stand, a playground, a theatre for marionettes, a merry-go-round, boules pitches, deckchairs, orchards with 300 varieties of apple, and an apiary, where you can take courses in beekeeping.

Food and Drink

❶ CAFÉ DE FLORE

172 boulevard St-Germain, 6th; tel: 01 45 48 55 26; daily 7am–2am; €€€
Grand historic café with Art Deco interior. In the days when it was less expensive, it was frequented by Jean-Paul Sartre and Simone de Beauvoir.

❷ LES DEUX MAGOTS

6 place St-Germain-des-Prés, 6th; tel: 01 45 48 55 25; daily 7.30am–1am; €€€
Rival to Café de Flore, and also once habituated by Sartre and de Beauvoir, as well as Hemingway, Picasso and Gide, among others. Like many places that have become an institution, it is also now pretty expensive and can get very busy. Light food.

❸ AU PETIT SUISSE

16 rue de Vaugirard, 6th; tel: 01 43 26 03 81; €
Unpretentious café with terrace. Snacks served noon till midnight.

Art Nouveau Abbesses metro station

MONTMARTRE

Romantic relic of a simpler, more vital world or clichéd victim of its own success? Approach Montmartre with a fresh mind and steer clear of the obvious tourist traps, and you will find plenty here to engage and surprise.

> **DISTANCE:** 3.5km (2.25 miles)
> **TIME:** A full day
> **START:** Les Abbesses
> **END:** Place de Clichy
> **POINTS TO NOTE:** Montmartre's streets are very steep, so this is not the best route if you prefer easy walks on the flat. (Taking the funicular up the hill will take some strain out of the climb.)

Montmartre has always stood slightly apart from the rest of the city. For much of the 19th century it was mined for gypsum and still retained a country charm with its vineyards, cornfields, flocks of sheep and 40 windmills. The lofty isolation of the hill and its cheap lodgings attracted artists, such as Toulouse-Lautrec, and writers. Painters and their models frequented place Pigalle (the red-light district), and people flocked to the Moulin Rouge. Impressionism, Fauvism and Cubism were conceived in the area's garrets, bars and dance halls.

LES ABBESSES

At the exit of metro Les Abbesses, note the Art Nouveau canopy by Hector Guimard, one of only two (the other is at place Dauphine) in the city to survive. Opposite is another Art Nouveau structure: **St-Jean de Montmartre** ❶. Built 1897–1904 to designs by Anatole de Baudot, the church is an early example of construction with reinforced cement and brick. Inside are several wall paintings (unfinished) executed at the end of World War I and depicting the Gospel of St-John.

Now, making a mental note that nearby is **Rose Bakery**, see ①, a good lunch option for later, head east off the square on rue Yvonne Le Tac. At no. 9 is the **Chapelle du Martyr** ❷, where, according to legend, St Denis, the first Bishop of Paris, picked up his head after being decapitated by the Romans in AD 287. He is then said to have walked off with it to where the basilica of St-Denis now stands 10km (6 miles) to the north. Montmartre means 'hill of the martyr'.

The Sacré-Cœur　　　　　　　　　　　*Capturing the view from La Butte*

PLACE ST-PIERRE

The road now becomes rue Tardieu and then place St-Pierre. With Montmartre's white basilica rising above you, walk to the far side of the place, where, on your left, is the **Halle St-Pierre**. This 19th-century covered market hall designed by Victor Baltard houses the **Musée de la Halle St-Pierre ❸** (Mon–Fri 10am–6pm, Sat until 7pm, Sun 11am–6pm, closed Sat–Sun in Aug; charge), which shows brut and naïve artworks by artists from around the world. It also hosts music concerts and lectures, and has an excellent bookshop and café.

Now either walk up through square Willette, laid out in terraces in 1929, or take the funicular railway (the fare is one metro ticket) to reach the terrace in front of Sacré-Cœur.

SACRÉ-CŒUR

Sacré-Cœur ❹ (35 rue Chevalier-de-la-Barre; www.sacre-coeur-montmartre.com; basilica: daily 6am–10.30pm, crypt and dome: summer 9am–7pm, winter 9am–6pm; entry to basilica

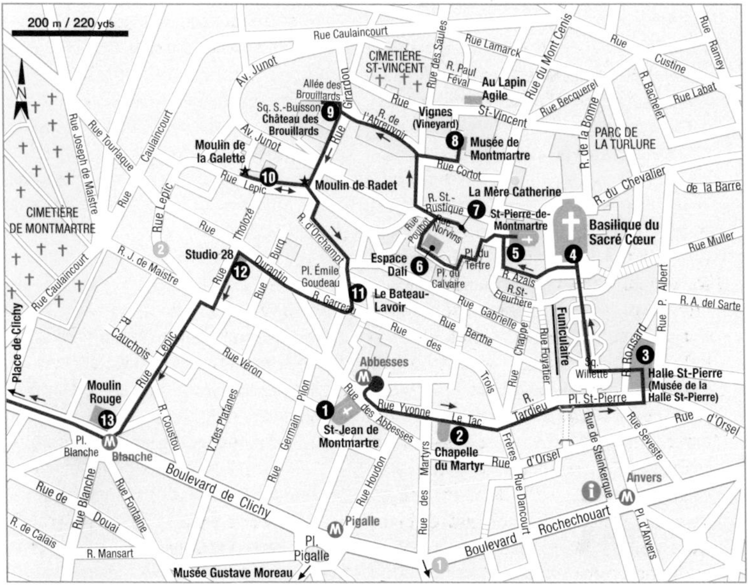

Street artists teem in Place du Tertre

free, charge for dome and crypt) was constructed after the suppression of the 1871 Paris Commune, which had been passionately supported by the anarchist Montmartrois. The church was built in appeasement for the bloodshed, and because of this, and its arguably rather mediocre architecture, has never been well-loved by residents. However, the steps in front afford one of the best views of Paris.

Work started on the basilica in 1875 and was not completed until 1914, and it was then not consecrated until 1919. The architect, Paul Abadie, based his design on the Romano-Byzantine cathedral of St-Front in Périgueux and used Château-Landon stone, which secretes calcite when it rains, bleaching the walls a bone-white colour.

The dome, up 237 narrow spiral steps, offers a wonderful view over Paris. There is also a huge bell, the Savoyarde, weighing 18 tonnes. From the stained-glass gallery beneath is a good view of the cavernous interior.

PLACE DU TERTRE

Now head west from the church on rue Azais and turn right on to rue St-Eleuthère to arrive at place du Tertre, which regrettably now has more than its fair share of overpriced restaurants and bad would-be artists. Stay briefly on the square, however, for a couple of more worthwhile sights.

St-Pierre de Montmartre

On your right is the simple church of **St-Pierre-de-Montmartre** ⑤ (daily 8.45am – 7pm; free), the second oldest in Paris (after St-Germain-des-Prés), dating from 1133, and all that remains of the old Abbey of Montmartre. A Benedictine nunnery since the 12th century, the abbey was destroyed during the Revolution. The church itself was then abandoned and only reconsecrated in 1908. It is noteworthy too that, according to the earliest biography of St-Ignatius Loyola, it was here that the vows were taken that led to the founding of the Jesuits.

Inside, the walls and columns (Roman in origin) of the nave seem to have bent with age and lean outwards. If you are here on Toussaint (All Saints' Day – 1 November), visit the small, romantic graveyard behind the church, since this is the only day of the year that it is open.

Dalí Museum

On the opposite side of the square is place du Calvaire, which forms a terrace with a fine view over Paris. At its far end, on the corner of rue Poulbot, is **Espace Dalí** ⑥ (11 rue Poulbot; www.daliparis.com; daily 10am – 6pm, July–Aug until 8pm; charge), with more than 300 works by the Surrealist artist.

The original bistro

Following rue Poulbot round, turn right at rue Norvins to reach 6 place du Tertre, home of **La Mère Catherine** ⑦,

Retro postcards for sale   *On the steps of St-Pierre-de-Montmartre*

reputedly Paris's first bistro. Originally a drinking den for revolutionaries, the old inn apparently served Russian soldiers during the Allied occupation of 1814. As they ordered their drinks – forbidden by the Russian military authorities – they shouted 'bistro' meaning 'quickly', thereby creating a Parisian institution.

Leaving the crowd of place du Tertre behind, head back to rue Norvins, then off onto rue des Saules where, at no. 22, is legendary cabaret **Au Lapin Agile** (www.au-lapin-agile.com; Tue–Sun 9pm–1am; charge). On wooden benches by scarred tables (though with original paintings by Gill and Léger), you are treated to a glass of cherries in *eau de vie* and a night of songs and poems in the tradition of Aristide Bruant. Once upon a time Renoir and Verlaine laid tables here, and Picasso paid for a day's meals with one of his *Harlequin* paintings: now worth millions of pounds.

Take the second right on to rue Cortot.

MUSÉE DE MONTMARTRE

At 12 rue Cortot, in the oldest house on the Butte, is the **Musée de Montmartre** ❶ (www.museedemontmartre. fr; daily 10am–6pm; charge), which chronicles the life and times of the artists' quarter.

This manor house was originally the country home of Rosimund, an actor in Molière's theatre company. Two hundred years later and the house had been divided into studios, with Renoir, Dufy, and Utrillo and his mother, Suzanne Valadon, living and working here. (Veladon's lover, the composer Erik Satie, lived in various lodgings on rue Cortot in the 1890s.)

The displays

Today, the lower floors are devoted to the history of Montmartre through revolutions and wars, whereas the upper floors evoke the bohemian artistic life of legend. As well as a reconstruction of Utrillo's favourite café, L'Abreuvoir, there is an artist's studio and artworks by Utrillo, Dufy and Toulouse-Lautrec. The gardens, where Renoir used to paint, are a peaceful oasis.

VINEYARD

Behind the museum are vineyards that were planted in 1933 in homage to the vines cultivated here since the Middle Ages. In early October, the grape harvest attracts hundreds of volunteers, and processions and parties take place in the neighbouring streets. About 300 litres (634 pints) of wine are sold at auction, with proceeds going to the Montmartre Festival Committee.

CASTLE OF THE MISTS

On the other side of rue des Saules from rue Cortot is rue de l'Abreuvoir, which becomes the allée des Brouillards. Here, **square Suzanne-Buisson** occu-

La Maison Rose, loved by Maurice Utrillo

pies the former gardens of the **Château des Brouillards 9**, which stands opposite. The house was built in 1772 and takes its name from the windmill that was here before and could only be seen when the fog lifted. Converted outhouses in its grounds were once inhabited by Renoir and the Symbolist poet Gérard de Nerval. Later the château became a dance hall, and then a squat before being restored.

RENOIR'S WINDMILL

Turn south on rue Girardon, then right on to rue Lepic. On your right is the **Moulin de la Galette 10**. Built in 1604, the windmill became a dance hall in the 19th century and was immortalised by Renoir in his 1866 painting of the same name.

BATEAU-LAVOIR

Now go back to rue Girardon, noting the other windmill here, the Moulin de Radet. Head south along the narrow rue d'Orchampt and continue to its end and place Émile-Goudeau. At no. 13, recently built artists' studios stand in place of the wooden ramshackle building in which Braque and Picasso invented Cubism. **Le Bateau-Lavoir 11**, so named because it resembled a floating laundry, was where Picasso painted *Les Demoiselles d'Avignon* (1907), recalling the prostitutes of Barcelona; in rooms alongside, Apollinaire and Max Jacob developed their

liberated verse-form. Sadly, the building burnt down in 1970 just as it was about to be renovated.

STUDIO 28

Turn right on to rue Garreau, which soon becomes rue Durantin, and, at the crossroads with rue Tholozé, turn left.

On your left is the famous cinema, **Studio 28 12**, where, in 1930, Luis Buñuel's *L'Age d'Or* (The Golden Age) caused a riot on only its second screening due to its overtly sexual content (the film only got past its censors through its being excused as 'the dream of a mad man'). Members of the fascist League

The New Athens

In the mid-19th century, the area south of boulevard de Clichy now known as La Nouvelle Athènes (New Athens) attracted writers, artists, composers, actresses and courtesans. For a sniff of this rarefied past, visit the Musée Gustave Moreau (14 rue de La Rochefoucauld; www.musee-moreau.fr; Mon, Wed, Thu 10am–12.45pm, 2–5.15pm, Fri–Sun 10am–5.15pm; charge) with its lovely double-height studio packed with Symbolist paintings, or the Musée de la Vie Romantique (right) at 16 rue Chaptal (Tue–Sun 10am–6pm; charge) with its memorabilia on the novelist George Sand and her circle of friends, including her lover the composer Chopin.

The singer Dalida lived here

The Moulin Rouge – you can't miss it

of Patriots threw ink at the screen, attacked members of the audience, and destroyed art work by Dalí, Miró, Man Ray, Yves Tanguy and others on display in the lobby. The film was subsequently banned for 50 years.

Rue Lepic

At the end of rue Tholozé, turn right, and soon after join the lower reaches of rue Lepic. No. 54 was home to Vincent Van Gogh and his brother Theo for two years in the late 1880s. At no. 42 is **À la Pomponette**, see ②, while at no. 15 is **Les Deux Moulins**, where Amélie Poulain waited on tables in the eponymous film. At the bottom of rue Lepic, turn right on to boulevard de Clichy.

PIGALLE

At the bottom of the Butte is **Pigalle**, or 'Pig Alley', as it was known to American soldiers during World War II. Once known exclusively for being the city's seedy red-light district, the area is cleaning up its act and is in parts now edgily cool. Some sex shops and seedy nightspots are still in evidence, but many of the old brothels and erotic cabarets are being replaced by trendy clubs (such as the Divan du Monde at 75 rue des Martyrs), chic boutiques and fashionable bars and restaurants.

The Moulin Rouge

Coming down the boulevard de Clichy, almost immediately on your right is the

Moulin Rouge ⑬ (82 boulevard de Clichy; www.moulinrouge.fr; charge), where a troupe of scantily clad 'Doriss' dancers delight spectators with their nightly show.

The club's history is gloriously scandalous. In 1896, the annual Paris Art School Ball was held here and featured the first fully nude striptease, by one of the school's models. She was arrested and imprisoned, and students went to the barricades in the Latin Quarter, proclaiming 'the battle for artistic nudity'.

Sparing a thought for the poet Jacques Prévert, who used to live just next door, now continue down the boulevard de Clichy towards place de Clichy, where the **Wepler**, see page 119, an old-world brasserie, forms a fitting end to this tour.

Food and Drink

❶ ROSE BAKERY

46 rue des Martyrs, 18th; tel: 01 42 82 12 80; Tue–Sat 9am–6.30pm; €–€€
Hip Franco-British café which serves savoury snacks, including quiches and salads, and yummy cakes to eat in or take away. A good option for vegetarians, there is also a branch in the Marais (30 rue Debelleyme, 3rd).

❷ À LA POMPONETTE

42 rue Lepic, 18th; tel: 01 46 06 08 36; daily lunch and dinner; €€€
Family-run bistro offering excellent renditions of classic French dishes.

Asian sculptures in Musée Guimet

TROCADÉRO

This walk to the Trocadéro in the 16th offers a varied selection of Parisian museums. Art or fashion, Asian antiquities or naval history: choose carefully which ones to visit, since to see them all would be exhausting.

> **DISTANCE:** 1.25km (0.75 mile)
> **TIME:** Half a day
> **START:** Place de l'Alma
> **END:** Palais de Chaillot
> **POINTS TO NOTE:** The time above includes the walk and two museum stops.

Start at place de l'Alma, and look out for la Flamme, a counterpart to the flame of the Statue of Liberty (gifted to the US by France). Then head west up avenue du Président Wilson. On your left, at no. 13, is the **Palais de Tokyo ❶**, built, along with the nearby Palais de Chaillot, for the 1937 World Fair and now home to two museums.

The **Musée d'Art Moderne de la Ville de Paris** (www.mam.paris.fr; Tue–Sun 10am–6pm; free except exhibitions), the municipal collection of modern art, is notable for Matisse's *La Danse* (1932) and Raoul Dufy's *Fée de l'Electricité* (Electricity Fairy) mural.

In the opposite wing is the **Site de Création Contemporaine** (www.palaisdetokyo.com; Wed–Mon noon–midnight; charge). Described as a 'laboratory for contemporary art', it reopened in 2012 after tripling its exhibition space and focuses on young artists. There is also a fashionable restaurant here, **Monsieur Bleu**, see ❶.

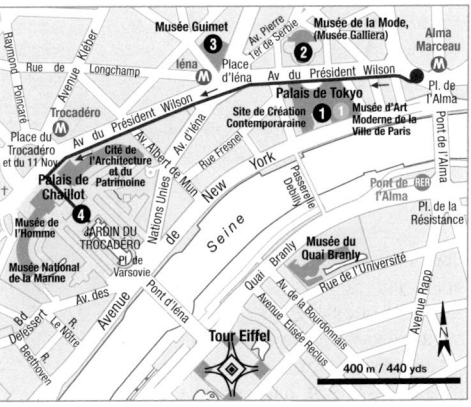

The imposing Art Deco Musée de l'Homme

MUSÉE DE LA MODE

On the other side of the road, in a mansion built by Gustave Eiffel, is the fashion museum, the **Musée de la Mode – Musée Galliera ❷** (10 avenue Pierre-1er-de-Serbie; daily Tue–Sun 10am–6pm when exhibitions are on only; charge). Drawing on its collection of 12,000 outfits and 60,000 accessories from the 18th century to the present, it shows two exhibitions each year.

MUSÉE GUIMET

Continuing along avenue du Président Wilson, you come to place d'Iéna where, at no. 6, is the **Musée National des Arts Asiatiques – Musée Guimet ❸**, the national museum of Asian art (Wed–Mon 10am–6pm; charge). It was founded in 1889 as a museum of world religions by Émile Guimet, a 19th-century industrialist and traveller. With the addition of the Oriental collections from the Louvre, it now owns 45,000 items. Highlights include the Treasure of Begram from Afghanistan and the Giant's Way, part of the temple complex from Angkor Wat, Cambodia.

PALAIS DE CHAILLOT

Continuing west for a further five minutes brings you to place du Trocadéro and the **Palais de Chaillot ❹**. This huge Art Deco complex contains three museums and a theatre. Major renovations are ongoing, so sections may be inaccessible.

First on your left is the **Cité de l'Architecture et du Patrimoine** (www.citechaillot.fr; Mon, Wed, Fri–Sun 11am–7pm, Thu 11am–9pm; charge), housing the world's largest museum dedicated to architecture, charting France's architectural history from cathedral portals and stained glass to Renaissance fountains and contemporary buildings.

In the west wing is the **Musée National de la Marine** (www.musee-marine.fr; Mon, Wed–Fri 11am–6pm, Sat–Sun until 7pm; charge). Displays of cannon barrels, early torpedoes, uniforms and paintings take you from ancient galleons to nuclear submarines.

Also in the west wing is the **Musée de l'Homme**, although this museum is closed for renovation until 2015.

Finish the route by walking down the steps behind the Palais de Chaillot to the gardens with their magnificent views of the Eiffel Tower.

Food and Drink

❶ MONSIEUR BLEU
Palais de Tokyo, avenue du Président-Wilson, 8th; tel: 01 47 20 90 47; daily noon–2am; €€€
Design-conscious and fun, this restaurant has a traditional menu and a terrace with views over the Eiffel Tower. There's also **Tokyo Eat** (tel: 01 47 20 00 29; closed Tue), which has a mix of Japanese and French cuisine with veggie options.

Statue of a praying girl in Père Lachaise

PÈRE LACHAISE

Wander in the maze of celebrity graves at Père Lachaise, then walk through Belleville, which, once a country village, then a workers' district, now offers an understated mix of cafés, artists' collectives, cottages and gardens.

DISTANCE: 4km (2.5 miles)
TIME: Half a day
START: Père Lachaise
END: Place du Colonel Fabien
POINTS TO NOTE: The best metro station for the start of this tour is Philippe Auguste.

From metro Philippe Auguste, turn right on to boulevard de Ménilmontant for Paris's smartest address for the dead, the cemetery of **Père Lachaise** ❶ (www.pere-lachaise.com; daily 8am– 6pm, Sat from 8.30am, Sun from 9am; free). 'Residents' include Chopin, Molière and Rossini, as well as more recent luminaries: Edith Piaf, Gertrude Stein, Oscar Wilde, Jim Morrison and Yves Montand. At the main entrance on boulevard de Ménilmontant, visitors can pick up free maps pinpointing the more famous graves.

The cemetery is named after the confessor of Louis XIV, Père La Chaise, who lived in a Jesuit house here. In 1804 it was established as a cemetery by Napoleon, although it was initially deemed too far from the city to attract many burials. As a marketing ploy, the administrators organised the transfer of the remains of writers La Fontaine and Molière, and, later, lovers Héloïse and Abélard.

CEMETERY TOUR

Walk up avenue Principale and turn right on to avenue du Puits to find the tomb of Abélard and Héloïse. In the 12th century, Héloïse was a student of the controversial theologian, Abélard, and secretly became his lover and wife. Her father's fury ended in Abélard being castrated and banished to a monastery, and Héloïse forced into a convent. However, they have left to posterity their letters, professing a pure and faithful love.

Artists and writers
Retrace your steps to avenue Principale and make your way past the graves of Colette, Rossini and Alfred de Musset, up the shady paths to the chapel on the hilltop.

Continue in the same direction, on avenue des Combattants Étrangers morts pour la France, passing the grave of the spiritualist Allan Kardec and on to the grand crematorium, bordered by the graves of Isadora Duncan, Maria Callas, Max Ophuls and Max Ernst. From here, it is only a short walk to an exit gate or, if you are ready for more, take a right turn along avenue Circulaire to the top (eastern) corner of the cemetery and the Mur des Fédérés.

Mur des Fédérés

This wall was where the last 147 anarchist rebels of the Paris Commune, a courageous uprising against Prussian domination in 1871, were lined up and shot after their final resistance among the graves the night before. The bullet holes are still visible. Also here is the Jardin du Souvenir, home to many monuments commemorating the dead of World War II.

Lunch stop

Leaving the cemetery behind via the exit nearest the crematorium, you emerge on to rue des Rondeaux. Turn left towards Gambetta metro station, left again on to place Martin Nadaud and then look for **rue Sorbier** where you can lunch at **Le Rez-de-Chaussée**, see ❶.

BELLEVILLE

The tour now continues into **Belleville**. In the early 19th century, this was a fertile country village but in the second half it evolved into a poor working-class area and a forge of class agitation.Today the *quartier* is subject to gentrification, complete with the usual

Relaxing in the Parc de Belleville

transient symptoms of art collectives and small-scale impromptu galleries.

Passage Plantin

Cross over rue de Ménilmontant on to rue Henri Chevreau, after looking left to take in the view towards the Centre Pompidou. Follow the road as it veers to the left and then turn right at rue des Couronnes, and then left down an alley, **Passage Plantin ❷**, with pretty houses that were typical of Belleville before the property developers moved in.

Parc de Belleville

At the other end of Passage Plantin, turn left on rue du Transvaal, which soon becomes rue Piat. Here, there is a fine view over the **Parc de Belleville ❸** (8 or 9am–5.45pm in winter, 9.30pm in summer; free) and the wider city. The park cascades down the hillside, and is most attractive in its lowest reaches.

Rue Rébeval

Continue on rue Piat until you reach rue de Belleville. Just before you cross over on to rue Rébeval, look for no. 72, outside which singer Edith Piaf was supposed to have been born under a lamp-post.

On rue Rébeval, watch out for the quirky brick building at nos 78–80, on the left-hand side. Although now the Paris-Belleville School of Architecture, this was once the Meccano factory and the source of many a child's constructive Christmas presents.

Butte Bergeyre

At this point, turn right on to rue Pradier, then left again on to avenue Simon-Bolivar, which leads to the corner of the **Parc des Buttes-Chaumont ❹** (see page 78).

Follow the western edge of the park on rue Manin and turn left down avenue Mathurin Moreau. On the left-hand side is the **Butte Bergeyre ❺**, which before World War I was the site of a fairground. It is now a quaint complex of lanes, houses and gardens clinging to the hillsides.

Place du Colonel Fabien

Rue Mathurin Moreau leads to place du Colonel Fabien, named after the *nom de guerre* of the French Communist resistance hero, Pierre Georges. Fittingly, the square is now dominated by the headquarters of the French Communist Party in a Modernist building designed by Brazilian architect Oscar Niemeyer.

To return to central Paris, pick up the metro at Colonel-Fabien, nearby.

Food and Drink

❶ LE REZ-DE-CHAUSSÉE

10 rue Sorbier, 20th; tel: 01 43 58 30 14; €€

Simple French classics are this friendly bistro's best offerings: oeuf en cocotte, faux filet, mousse au chocolat. Great value.

The Canal is just as atmospheric at night

NORTHEAST PARIS

Catch a boat, cycle or stroll up the canal to an often-overlooked area of Paris that has lots to appeal to both children and adults: a science museum, 3-D cinema, submarine, music museum, beautiful parks and spectacular city views.

DISTANCE: 9km (6.5 miles)
TIME: A full day
START: Place de la Bastille
END: Parc des Buttes-Chaumont
POINTS TO NOTE: If you choose to cycle up the canal, you can pick up a Vélib' bike (see page 124) at place de la Bastille or place de la République.

The route begins by following the Canal St-Martin from **place de la Bastille ❶** up to the northeast of Paris. Either start early and board a Canauxrama tour boat (www.canauxrama.com; reservations essential; charge), or cycle or stroll up the canal towpaths.

CANAL CRUISE

If you choose the boat, the 2.5-hour cruise begins at the **Arsenal Marina ❷** (once a busy commercial port), by 50 boulevard de la Bastille. Departures are at 9.45am and 2.30pm daily, and commentaries are in both English and French. Sit on the top deck for the best views. (Note that cruises also run in the opposite direction.)

Going underground

Napoleon commissioned the canal partly to allow more water into the city centre and earn the citizens' affection.

At place de la Bastille, the canal goes underground, emerging again beyond **place de la République ❸**. As you glide under the city, you pass through a strip of the canal that is lit by pavement gratings that send shafts of light down to the water. The different colours of mortar indicate where restoration work has been carried out; the area overhead has been untouched since the canal was built.

Hôtel du Nord

At **quai de Valmy** and **quai de Jemmapes**, you emerge amid trees and gardens into a unique Parisian landscape, punctuated with 19th-century iron footbridges and locks. On the right bank is the **Hôtel du Nord ❹**, the inspiration for Marcel Carné's 1938 film of the same name, and now an atmospheric bar and

The Canal sees a lot of boat traffic

bistro. In the evenings, it is a venue for Anglophone stand-up comedy.

Behind it is the **Hôpital St-Louis** ⑤, built from 1607 to shelter plague victims. Adjacent, on rue de la Grange-aux-Belles, are two noteworthy *chanson* cafés for evening wine and song, Chez Adel (no. 10) and Apostrophe (no. 23).

Back on quai de Valmy, at no. 200, is one of the city's foremost alternative cultural venues, the **Point Ephémère** (www.point ephemere.org). A 1930s former warehouse, it has been converted into artists' studios, a club, music studios, a gallery and a café. Another nice café on quai de Valmy is **Chez Prune**, see ①.

Rotonde de la Villette

Going north, at place de Stalingrad you reach the **Rotonde de la Villette** ⑥, one of Claude Nicholas Ledoux's beautifully designed tollhouses (now hosting exhibitions). It marks the start of the **Bassin de la Villette**, built for Napoleon in 1808, and bordered by stylish new cinemas, beautiful old warehouses

and some less appealing 1960s and '70s high-rise blocks. In true post-industrial fashion, some warehouses here have been reclaimed by artists' cooperatives as studio space.

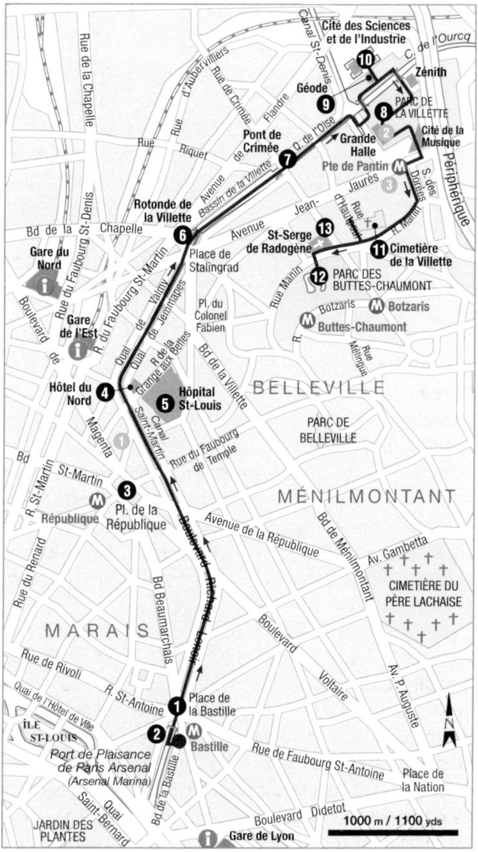

Canal views

'Pocket submarine' at the Cité des Sciences

At the top end of the basin is an ingenious piece of 19th-century engineering: a hydraulic lifting bridge, the **Pont de Crimée ❼**, which displaces a whole section of road. Just beyond the port is the Parc de la Villette, where the canal divides into the canals de l'Ourcq and St-Denis, and where the boat ride comes to an end.

PARC DE LA VILLETTE

The **Parc de la Villette ❽** (avenues Corentin-Cariou and Jean-Jaurès; www.villette.com; daily; free) was created in 1986 as one of François Mitterrand's *grands projets* (see page 30), on a 50-ha (136-acre) site, where the city's meat market once stood.

Géode
On the left of the canal is the **Géode ❾**, a polished-steel sphere, which looks rather like something from outer space. Inside, the hemispheric theatre has one of the world's largest screens and dizzily slanted seating. Movies are made specially for this huge screen, many on a natural science theme.

Cité des Sciences
The **Cité des Sciences et de l'Industrie ❿** (www.cite-sciences.fr; Tue–Sat 10am–6pm, Sun 10am–7pm; charge except for ground-floor exhibits in main hall), or science museum, was created from the shell of an unfinished slaughterhouse building.

Inside, there is plenty to see, particularly for children (of all ages): try out the jet-pack simulator for armchair astronauts, experience the sensations of space sickness or weightlessness, practise on a flight simulator, and perform experiments using mirrors, electricity and tricks of perspective. There are other exhibits on the origins of life, the underwater world, plant life, and there are even robotic animals in a cybernetic zoo.

The **Planétarium** runs several programmes a day. There is an extra charge for these: buy your tickets as soon as you arrive, since they sell out quickly.

The **Cité des Enfants** has lots of fun, interactive attractions for children, with areas divided according to age (2–7 and 5–12 year olds).

The park
The park itself is the largest in Paris, spread over more than 35ha (86 acres). It was designed by Swiss landscape architect Bernard Tschumi as 15 gardens, each with a different theme. Children should enjoy the Dragon's Garden, the Garden of the Winds and the Garden of Childhood Fears, with its fairy-tale mystery, dark colours and engaging sound system. Adults may prefer the subtlety of the Garden of Shadows and the beauty of the Garden of Bamboos.

In summer, the Triangle Meadow is a nice place to sit and enjoy a picnic. You can even watch an outdoor movie here, on a giant inflatable screen.

The Géode at the Parc de la Villette

At regular intervals in the park, you will spot bright-red enamelled-steel buildings, which are contemporary versions of 18th-century French architectural fantasies or follies. Each one looks different and is devoted to a special activity; the Folie Argonaute, for example, leads you to a real submarine that arrived via the Canal de l'Ourcq.

Zénith

Next to the northern bridge is a large, grey, solid-looking tent, the **Zénith**, a concert hall that can seat up to 6,300 people and is best known as the centre of Paris's thriving rap scene. Opposite, a new-wave circus performs below the big top of **Espace Chapiteaux**.

On the east side of the canal is **La Grande Halle**, a fine example of 19th-century iron architecture. Until 1974 it housed France's national meat market, but it was rendered obsolete by modern refrigeration and poor design – the cows could not get up the steps – and is now an exhibition space with a hip café-bar, **La Villette Enchantée**, see ❷. Shows range from the prestigious, often controversial Paris Biennale contemporary art show to the International Architectural Fair, to fashion shows. Nearby is the **Maison de la Villette**, home to an exhibition on the history of the park.

Cité de la Musique

On the extreme southeastern edge of the park is the **Cité de la Musique**. Designed by architect Christian de

Portzamparc, the complex includes the **Musée de la Musique** (www.citedela musique.fr; Tue–Sat noon–6pm, Sun 10am–6pm; charge). The museum charts the development of classical, jazz and folk music and houses an impressive collection of more than 4,500 musical instruments. On the other side of the Grande Halle is Portzamparc's Conservatoire, where you can attend concerts by top performers.

CIMETIÈRE DE LA VILLETTE

Leaving La Cité de la Musique and Parc de la Villette, cross avenue Jean-Jaurès (perhaps stopping for lunch at the epicure's valhalla, **Au Bœuf Couronné**, see ❸). Note that there is a pick-up/drop-off point (Station Vélib') for city bikes on Jean-Jaurès at this point.

Head down Sente des Dorées and then take the second right on to rue Manin for the pleasant 15-minute walk to the Parc des Buttes-Chaumont. On the way, a minor detour on to rue d'Haut-poul on your right brings you to the **Cimetière de la Villette** ⓫ (mid-Mar–Oct 8am–6pm, Nov–mid-Mar 8am–5.30pm; free). Through a monumental gateway you find a mini version of Père Lachaise cemetery with huge 19th-century tombs set under a canopy of trees.

PARC DES BUTTES-CHAUMONT

The **Parc des Buttes-Chaumont** ⓬ (daily: Oct–Apr 7am–8pm, May–Aug

Musée de la Musique guitars · *Parc des Buttes-Chaumont*

7am–10pm, Sept 7am–9pm; free), one of the finest parks in Paris, was built by Baron Haussmann in the 1860s on the site of a rubbish dump and gypsum quarry. The uneven ground provided a perfect setting for a wooded, rocky terrain, and a lake has been created around an artificial 50m (165ft) 'mountain', which is capped by a Roman-style temple, with a waterfall and a cave containing fake stalactites. Ice-skating, and boating are also on offer, and the puppet show or 'Guignols' in the open-air theatre has been a popular attraction for more than 150 years (weather permitting, shows are on Wed, Sat and Sun at 4pm and 5pm).

Russian church

On the western side of the park, near where you entered, is the atmospheric Russian church of **St-Serge-de-Radogène** ⑬ (irregular opening hours; free). You approach it through a gateway at 93 rue de Crimée. Originally built as a Protestant church in 1861, it was acquired by the Russian Orthodox Church in 1924 to minister to the influx of Russian immigrants fleeing the Revolution.

BACK TO CENTRAL PARIS

To get back into town from here, you can take the metro from Buttes-Chaumont or Botzaris. Alternatively, take bus no. 75, which goes to the Centre Pompidou and Hôtel de Ville. The bus begins back at place de la Porte de Pantin, near where you left the Parc de la Villette, but has various stops at points around Parc des Buttes-Chaumont. It only runs until about 10.30pm.

Food and Drink

① CHEZ PRUNE

36 rue Beaurepaire, 10th; tel: 01 42 41 30 47; Mon–Sat 8am–2am, Sun 10am–2am; €

Watch the world go by at this cornerstone of trendy Canal St-Martin. Respectable food at lunch time and tapas-style snacks at night.

② LA VILLETTE ENCHANTÉE

211 avenue de Jean-Jaurès, 19th; tel: 01 40 35 96 49; daily 11am–8pm, food served until 4pm; €€

Opposite the Cité de la Musique in La Grande Halle, this fashionable café and club (Fri–Sat) is a popular place for brunch at weekends. Lovely terrace.

③ AU BŒUF COURONNÉ

188 avenue Jean-Jaurès, 19th; tel: 01 42 39 44 44; daily; €€€

Outstanding restaurant just across the road from where the meat market (now the music Conservatoire) used to be. Specialises in butchery: every kind of steak, bone marrow with toast and *tête de veau* (veal's head). Not for the fainthearted.

Boating in the Bois de Vincennes

BERCY AND VINCENNES

Follow a pretty garden path along a former railway viaduct towards the regeneration quarter of Bercy. Choose between exploring the Bois de Vincennes or the old centre of the wine trade with its bars, cafés, cinemas and park.

DISTANCE: 7.25km (4.5 miles)
TIME: Half a day
START: Opéra Bastille
END: Parc de Vincennes or Bercy

Starting at the **Opéra National de la Bastille ❶**, walk down rue de Lyon and take avenue Daumesnil on your left. You will soon reach some steps, signposted Promenade Plantée. At the top begins a walk along a former railway viaduct now transformed into a garden.

Underneath the arches, dubbed the **Viaduc des Arts ❷** (15–121 avenue Daumesnil), are the shops of artisans and café **L'Arrosoir**, see ❶. At the end of the promenade is the **Jardin de Reuilly ❸**.

At this point, you have a choice: either continue along avenue Daumesnil to the Bois de Vincennes, or head south to the Parc de Bercy and Bercy Village.

BOIS DE VINCENNES

If heading for the Bois de Vincennes, continue along avenue Daumesnil until you come to the **Palais de la Porte Dorée ❹** (Tue–Fri 10am–5.30pm, Sat–Sun 10am–7pm; charge) at no. 293, with its extraordinary basement aquarium and

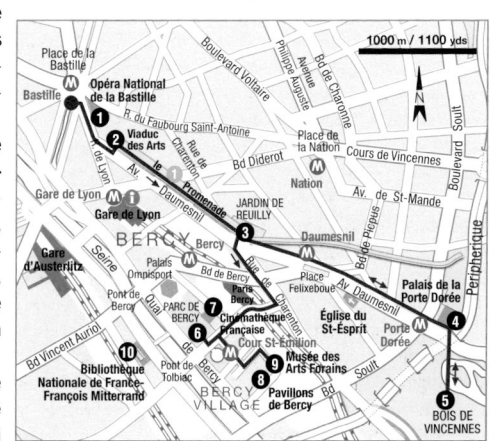

Inside the Musée des Arts Forains

a cultural institute on the role of immigrants in France over the last 200 years.

Bois de Vincennes and Parc Floral
Continue on avenue Daumesnil to the **Bois de Vincennes ❺** (daily dawn–dusk; free), Paris's largest green space. Attractions include boating, cycle paths, a Buddhist temple, zoo (closed for renovation until 2014), hippodrome and theatre. The **Parc Floral** (charge) inside has a playground and crazy golf.

Château de Vincennes
On the northern edge of the park is the **Château de Vincennes** (www.chateau-vincennes.fr; 23 Sept–20 May: daily 10am–5pm, 21 May–22 Sept until 6pm; charge), completed by Charles V in 1370 and now housing a museum.

BERCY

For the alternative option of **Bercy Village**, bear right after the Jardin de Reuilly on to rue de Charenton, and turn right on to rue Prudhon. Follow the road over the railway, past the church and on to the **Parc de Bercy ❻** (May–Aug: Mon–Fri 8am–9.30pm, Sat–Sun 9am–9.30pm; Mar–Apr, Sept: Mon–Fri 8am–8.30pm, Sat–Sun 9am–8.30pm, Oct until 7.30pm, Nov–Feb until 6.30pm; free).

At the western end of the park is the rather ugly Ministère de l'Economie et du Budget and the Palais Omnisports, a stadium and events venue. Also within the park is the Frank Gehry-designed

Cinémathèque Française ❼ (51 rue de Bercy; www.cinemathequefrancaise. com; daily except Tue, see website for times): a film museum and film archive.

Bercy Village
As late as the 1980s wine was unloaded from barges at Bercy. Forty-two *chais* (wine warehouses) have been cleaned up and reopened as restaurants, wine bars and shops, and some have been converted into the **Pavillons de Bercy ❽**, containing the **Musée des Arts Forains ❾** (by appointment only), home to a collection of fairground music and Venetian carnival salons.

'NEW' LEFT BANK

Opposite Bercy on the so-called 'New' Left Bank is the **Bibliothèque Nationale de France – François Mitterrand ❿**. Its four 90m (295ft) -high glass towers are intended to evoke open books. The regenerated area is now home to many attractive bars and cafés, including several riverside ones.

> ## Food and Drink
>
> **❶ L'ARROSOIR**
> 75 avenue Daumesnil, 12th; tel: 01 43 43 64 58; open daily; €€
> Stylish café underneath the Viaduc des Arts, which is ideal for breakfast, brunch (Sat–Sun), lunch or dinner.

Musée du Vin cellars

WESTERN PARIS

This is a posh part of town and off the main tourist track. Its attractions include pretty parks, Art Nouveau and Modernist architecture, Balzac's house and museums of wine and Impressionist art.

> **DISTANCE:** 3.5km (2.25 miles)
> **TIME:** A full day
> **START:** Passy metro station
> **END:** Musée Marmottan or the Bois de Boulogne
> **POINTS TO NOTE:** If you end the tour after the Musée Marmottan, pick up the metro at La Muette; if you continue to the Bois de Boulogne, the metro is at Porte Dauphine and Porte d'Auteuil.

The 16th *arrondissement* constitutes a sizeable slice of western Paris and is full of smart residences occupied by wealthy inhabitants. Just adjacent (though outside the Périphérique) is the Bois de Boulogne, an 860-ha (2,125-acre) expanse of woods and gardens laid out under town planner Baron Haussmann.

MUSÉE DU VIN

Catch the metro to Passy, and, as you leave the station, turn right down the steps. Turn right again at the bottom, then right a third time at rue des Eaux. This street is named after the mineral springs where people came to take cures for anaemia in the days when Passy was a country village. Ironically, at the end of this street, at no. 5 square Charles-Dickens, is the **Musée du Vin** ❶ (www.museeduvinparis.com; Tue–Sun 10am–6pm; charge).

Here, within the cellars of a wine-producing monastery destroyed in the Revolution, you are guided through the wine-making process. There are also regular wine tastings (some in English) and a restaurant (Tue–Sat lunch only).

As you leave, turn right on to rue Charles Dickens and walk straight on to the modest **Parc de Passy** ❷. Climb the steps on the north side of the park up to rue Raynouard and turn left.

MAISON DE BALZAC

On your left, at no. 47, is the **Maison de Balzac** ❸ (www.balzac.paris.fr; Tue–Sun 10am–6pm; permanent collection free). The writer Honoré de Balzac (1799–1850), a self-styled 'quill and

Bust of Balzac in his house-museum

ink galley slave', lived here in secret for seven years, from 1840 (under the assumed name of Monsieur Breugnol, one of the characters in his novels) in order to escape his creditors. On the simple table in his study he worked day and night on *La Comédie Humaine*, his vast series of 91 novels and stories peopled with thousands of interconnected characters.

RADIO FRANCE

Now continue in the same direction on rue Raynouard to the **Maison de Radio-France ❹** (entrance on far side, at 116 avenue du Président Kennedy; tours daily except Sun by reservation only; charge), the Orwellian home of the state radio station and broadcasting bureaucracy opened in 1963. Concerts, usually classical music, take place here every week.

ALTERNATIVE ROUTES

At this point you have a choice of routes. If you want to fast forward to the Musée Marmottan (see page 85), turn right and walk up rue du Ranelagh. At the end of the road, go through the passage and turn right over the zebra crossing to the Jardins du Ranelagh. The museum is on the left, just off avenue Raphael.

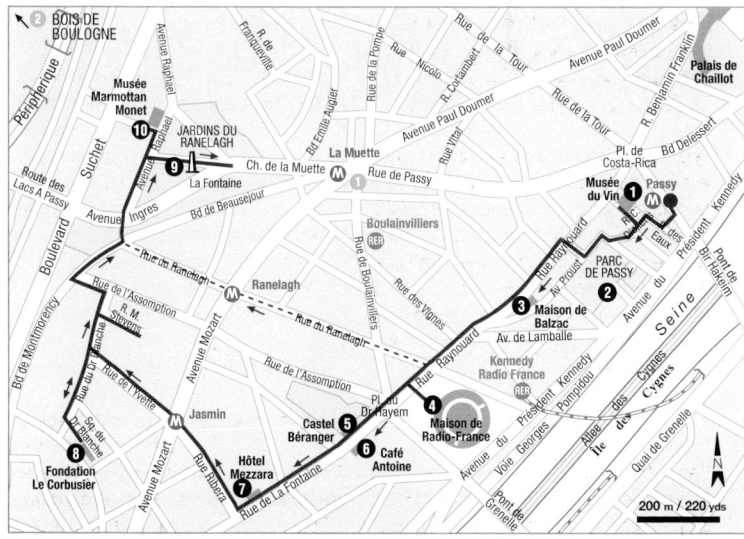

Guimard's elaborate Castel Béranger

If, on the other hand, you are interested in taking a detour for an hour or so in order to see some fine examples of Art Nouveau and Modernist architecture, go up rue La Fontaine.

ARCHITECTURE TOUR

Art Nouveau
Rue Jean de La Fontaine is home to the city's best examples of Art Nouveau architecture by Hector Guimard, the man who was responsible for the flamboyant entrances to metro stations such as the one at Abbesses (see page 64). On your right at no. 14 is the extraordinary **Castel Béranger** ❺, Guimard's first building commission, and he designed everything: the mosaic floors, the wallpaper, even the stoves. Despite its lavish decoration, Castel Béranger was built as a cheap lodging house.

Guimard also designed the more modest buildings at nos 19 and 21, and the tiny **Café Antoine** ❻ at no. 17 on your left. Further up, at no. 60, is **Hôtel Mezzara** ❼, whose wonderful interior steals the limelight from the free art exhibitions it hosts.

Soon after, turn right on to rue Ribera, which then becomes rue de l'Yvette.

Modernism
At the top of rue de l'Yvette is rue du Dr Blanche, with two examples of Modernist architecture. Turn left for square du Dr Blanche and the **Fondation Le Corbusier** ❽ (see box) on your left. Next, turn right, and on your right is rue Mallet-Stevens, almost entirely made up of houses by Robert Mallet-Stevens (1886–1945). No. 10, with its stained-glass stairwell, is very fine.

Now continue north up rue du Dr Blanche and turn left at rue de l'Assomption, and then right on boulevard de Montmorency. Soon on your left is an inconspicuous path taking you through to avenue Ingres. Turn right and over the zebra crossing you will find the **Jardins**

Le Corbusier

Although Charles-Edouard Jeanneret (1887–1965), known as Le Corbusier, developed his brand of Modernism to provide better living conditions for inhabitants of crowded cities, he has been criticised for inspiring the building of soulless tower blocks surrounded by featureless wastelands. However, the two adjoining houses that make up the **Fondation Le Corbusier** (8–10 square du Dr Blanche; www.fondationlecorbusier.asso.fr; Mon 1.30–6pm, Tue–Sat 10am–6pm; guided tours in English at 2pm on Tue; charge) show how elegant and light his buildings can be. Inside are exhibition spaces for his drawings, plans, furniture and paintings. It is also possible to visit his apartment in the nearby Immeuble Molitor (24 rue Nungesser et Coli, 16th; tel: 01 46 03 32 90; by appointment only Sat 10am–1pm, 1.30–5pm; charge).

House by Mallet-Stevens

The Marmottan showcases Monet's work

du Ranelagh ❾, an appealing park for young children, as it retains several old-fashioned carousels.

MUSÉE MARMOTTAN MONET

West of the gardens on the corner of rue Louis-Boilly (at no. 2) is the **Musée Marmottan Monet** ❿ (www.marmottan. com; Tue–Sun 10am–6pm, Thu until 8pm; charge), which gives an unrivalled overview of the career of Claude Monet (1840–1926). In the gallery downstairs, you start with *Impression, Soleil Levant (Impression, Sunrise)*, which gave the Impressionist Movement its name. Monet's ideas then evolve up to his last, almost abstract, *Nymphéas (Waterlily)* paintings.

Thanks to other donations, Monet's contemporaries are also well represented. On the first floor are works by Pissarro, Renoir, Manet, Morisot, Caillebotte and Gauguin. On the ground floor, slightly incongruously, there is a fine collection of First Empire furniture as well as a section on medieval illuminated manuscripts.

PARKS AND GARDENS

With the route nearing its end, you have a choice of walking back through the Ranelagh gardens to cafés, restaurants and the metro home, or strolling through the vast **Bois de Boulogne** (24 hours; free) to the west beyond the Marmottan.

For the first option, walk back towards town along chaussée de la Muette. On the way you pass the **statue of La Fontaine** with the fox and crow from one of his fables, and, as you leave the park, the lively **La Gare**, see ①.

Bois de Boulogne

For the second option, if it is a pleasant summer evening, consider a meal at **Le Chalet des Îles**, see ②. Otherwise, seek out **Les Serres d'Auteuil**, to the south (near the Roland Garros tennis centre). These romantic glasshouses, opened in 1895, offer seasonal displays of orchids and begonias as well as a tropical pavilion with palm trees, birds and a pool of Japanese carp.

Food and Drink

① LA GARE

19 chaussée de la Muette, 16th; tel: 01 42 15 15 31; daily; €€€

Former railway station, where the ticket office has become the bar, and the platforms dining areas. Good-value lunch menus and there's brunch on Sundays.

② LE CHALET DES ÎLES

Lac Inférieur, Bois de Boulogne, 16th; tel: 01 42 88 04 69; Tue–Sun (Sun lunch only) and Mon in summer; €€€€

A short boat ride to the island on the more northerly of the park's two lakes leads to this pretty chalet, transplanted from Switzerland by Napoleon III. Gorgeous setting.

The Grande Arche

LA DÉFENSE

Named after a stand against the Prussians in 1870, La Défense is now a business district dominated by the Grande Arche, which completes the Royal Axis that links the Louvre, Tuileries, Champs–Élysées and Arc de Triomphe.

DISTANCE: 1.5km (1 mile)
TIME: 3 hours
START: Les Quatre Temps Shopping Centre, La Défense
END: Espace Raymond Moretti
POINTS TO NOTE: Take RER line A or metro line 1 to La Défense-Grande Arche.

La Défense was designated a business district as early as 1958, but it was not until the 1980s that its reputation was secured. Nowadays, more than 180,000 people work in the district, and about three-quarters of the top 20 French companies have their headquarters here, as do around a dozen of the top 50 companies in the world. And even though La Défense was officially completed in 1988 after 20 years' work, many of the original buildings are now being replaced with more advanced constructions as part of a grand plan entitled 'La Défense 2006–2015'.

NEW DEVELOPMENTS

New buildings include the Hermitage Plaza, designed by Sir Norman Foster, which consist of two towers, one with 91 floors and the other with 89 floors, and will be the tallest building in the European Union at 323 metres (1059 ft) when it is completed in 2018. Tour Phare (Lighthouse Tower), designed by the American architect Thom Mayne, is expected to be completed in 2017 and will also consist of two buildings: a central tower of 297 metres (974 ft) and a lower trapezoidal building. And if other projects have been cancelled due to mounting costs, La Défense is nonetheless entering a new era.

Food and Drink

 **LE MOND**

1 place des Corolles, 92400 Courbevoie; tel: 01 47 75 97 11; Mon–Fri; €€€
Classy restaurant with a shaded summer terrace where the (mainly business) clientèle enjoys seasonal market cuisine.

Lunch on the Arche's steps　　　　　　　　　　　*Beneath the Arche*

GRANDE ARCHE

The metro exit brings you into **Les Quatre Temps** ❶ shopping centre. Follow signs to the **Grande Arche** ❷ (closed to the public since 2010 for safety reasons). More than any other building, it is this great behemoth, designed by Danish architect Johan Otto von Spreckelsen, that put La Défense on the map, and in so doing became a symbol of François Mitterrand's 'progressive vision for the 1980s'.

From the steps of the arch, you can take in the Royal Axis that runs straight to the Arc de Triomphe, heads along the Champs-Élysées and Tuileries, and ends at the Arc de Triomphe du Carrousel and the Louvre. The size of the arch is symbolic, measuring 100m by 100m (330 sq ft), the same dimensions as the Cour Carrée at the Louvre.

SCULPTURE PARK

Wander down from the Grande Arche. On your left as you head southeast is the vaulted **CNIT** ❸ (Centre National des Industries et des Techniques; 2 place de la Défense), a huge conference and exhibition centre.

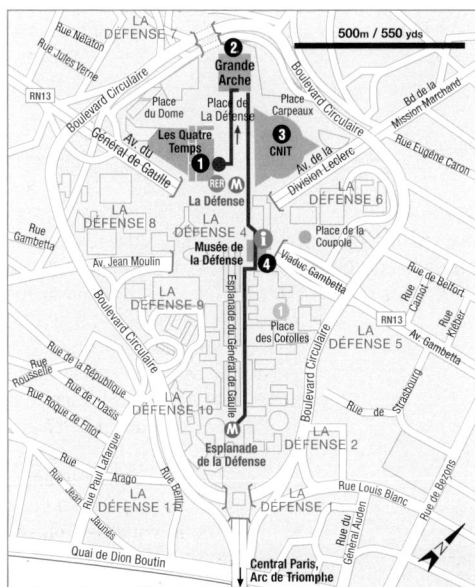

Next head for the tourist information centre on the esplanade du Général-de-Gaulle. In the basement is the **Musée de la Défense** ❹ (15 place de la Défense; www.ladefense.fr; daily 9am–5pm, Sat 10am–6pm; free), exploring 50 years of architectural innovation in this district. There is also an outdoor sculpture park, Le Musée à Ciel Ouvert, which includes works by Miró, César and Calder, as well as restaurant **Le Mond**, see ❶.

Continue down the esplanade du Général-de-Gaulle to take the metro back into central Paris.

Rear view of the exquisite château

MALMAISON

In the quiet suburb of Rueil–Malmaison is one of the most appealing châteaux within easy reach of the French capital: Malmaison, the stylish and evocative former home of Josephine Bonaparte, first wife of Napoleon I.

DISTANCE: 24km (15 miles) rtn
TIME: A full day
START: Château de Malmaison
END: Rueil-Malmaison
POINTS TO NOTE: The distance above is for the journey from Paris. By public transport take RER line A to La Défense-Grande Arche, then bus 258 to the 'Le Château' stop; by car, take RN 13 motorway from Paris.

To reach the **Château de Malmaison** ❶ (rue du Château; www.chateau-malmaison.fr; Wed–Mon Apr–Sept 10am–12.30pm, 1.30–5.45pm, Sat–Sun until 6.15pm, Oct–Mar 10am–12.30pm, 1.30–5.15pm, Sat–Sun until 5.45pm; charge), follow the instructions above.

BACKGROUND

The palace passed through various hands until, in 1799, it caught the eye of Madame Bonaparte. She engaged the services of up-and-coming architectural duo, Percier and Fontaine, to renovate the building in the fashionable neoclassical style, and in 1805 she employed L.M. Berthault to work on the park.

Country retreat and office

While Malmaison was initially used as a country retreat, by 1800 Napoleon was spending an increasing amount of time here. But in 1809, since Josephine could not provide an heir, Napoleon nullified the marriage and gave his former wife the Malmaison estate. She stayed here until her death in 1814.

TOUR OF THE CHÂTEAU

Highlights on the **ground floor** include a monumental billiard table, two paint-

Food and Drink

① LE BEAUHARNAIS

29 place de l'Eglise, RueilMalmaison; tel: 01 47 51 02 88; €
Nice brasserie in the church square with outdoor seating in summer.

Josephine and her children at Malmaison

ings by Gérard and Girodet and Josephine's harp topped by an Imperial eagle. Note also Napoleon's striped, tent-style council room and the library with its classical-style busts of authors from Ovid to Voltaire.

First and second floors

The **first floor** houses the private apartments, although little of what is now on display is original and comes from other former royal residences. Most striking are the paintings of the couple by artists Gérard, Riesener, Bacler d'Albe and David. The **second floor** is dedicated to Josephine's impressive wardrobe.

THE GARDEN

Walk round to the back of the building to admire the park, beautifully landscaped in the English country-garden style. Still here is the massive cedar tree planted in 1800 to celebrate Napoleon's victory over the Austrians at Marengo, in Italy. Napoleon's famous horse Marengo was named after the battle in which he carried his rider.

OTHER ATTRACTIONS

Tickets to Malmaison also cover entry to **Bois-Préau** (1 avenue de l'Impératrice Joséphine), although, at the time of writing, this château, now a Napoleonic museum, was closed for renovation.

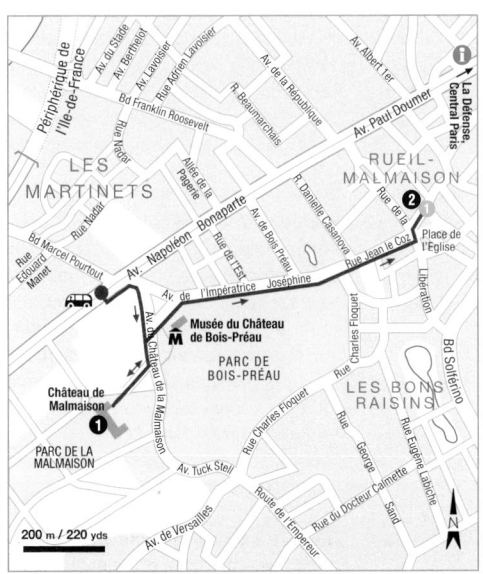

Also worth a pit stop are the **Pavillon Osiris** (Osiris Pavilion), with its decorative-arts collection, and the **Pavillon des Voitures** (Carriage Pavilion), showcasing Napoleon's field landau used in his Russian campaign and the hearse used on St-Helena for his funeral.

It is a 15-minute walk into little **Rueil-Malmaison ❷**, where Le Beauharnais, see ❶, is an inviting option.

Louis XIV, the Sun King

VERSAILLES

Described by the writer and philosopher Voltaire as 'a masterpiece of bad taste and magnificence', Versailles, symbol of pre-Revolutionary decadence, offers a vivid encounter with French history.

DISTANCE: 42km (26 miles) rtn
TIME: A full day
START/END: Versailles
POINTS TO NOTE: To reach the palace by public transport take the RER line C to Versailles-Rive-Gauche-Château. By car: Versailles is 21km (13 miles) southwest of Paris by the A13 autoroute; take the exit Versailles-Château. Park on place d'Armes.

To reach the palace of **Versailles** ❶ (www.chateauversailles.fr; Château: Apr–Oct Tue–Sun 9am–6.30pm, Nov–Mar Tue–Sun 9am–5.30pm. Petit Trianon, Hameau and Grand Trianon: Apr–Oct Tue–Sun noon–6.30pm, Nov–Mar Tue–Sun noon–5.30pm. Last entry 30 mins prior to closing. Gardens: Apr–Oct daily 8am–8.30pm, Nov–Mar daily 8am–6pm. Musical Fountains: Tue (mid-May–June), Sat and Sun (Mar–Oct). Musical Gardens: Tue (Apr–mid-May, Jul–Oct) from central Paris, follow the instructions above.

BEGINNINGS

In 1623, Louis XIII, a passionate hunts-man, built a lodge near the town of Ver-sailles to the west of Paris, in order to take advantage of the thick forest in the area. In 1631, the king instructed his architect to upgrade the lodge.

Louis XIV
From 1661–8 further changes were made under the young Louis XIV by archi-tect Louis Le Vau, painter Charles Leb-run and landscape gardener André Le Nôtre. Versailles was still too small, how-ever, for king and entourage, so in 1668 Louis commissioned Le Vau to envelop the existing palace in a new building. From 1678, Jules Hardouin-Mansart took over as main architect, heralding a period of prolific building.

Official court residence
In 1682 Versailles became Louis XIV's official residence and the seat of the French government. New construction included the Hall of Mirrors, North and South wings, Stables, Grand Lodgings,

The grand exterior of Versailles

The King's chief painter oversaw this ceiling painting

Orangery and Royal Chapel, as well as the redesign of the Grand Trianon.

Upon his proper accession to the throne after the Regency of 1715–22, Louis XV also kept court at Versailles. His architect, Ange-Jacques Gabriel, refurbished the private apartments and built the Petit Trianon (1762–4). Between 1768 and 1770 he also constructed the Royal Opera and in 1771 redesigned Mansart's crumbling North Wing in the classical French style.

REVOLUTION

The court under Louis XVI stayed at Versailles, keeping its distance from the increasingly discontented Parisian mob. This fantasy world was epitomised by the building of the Hameau (hamlet) for Marie-Antoinette between 1783 and 1787. Louis's world collapsed, however, when on 6 October 1789 he and his family were forced to return to the Palais des Tuileries in Paris. Louis, the last king in the Bourbon line, was guillotined on 21 January 1793.

NAPOLEON

After the Revolution, the palace was looted, and the estate fell into disrepair. Napoleon considered moving here, after his marriage in 1810 to his second wife, Archduchess Marie-Louise, but the plans never came to fruition. However, the couple did enjoy retreats in the Grand Trianon.

MUSEUM

Future occupants of the château did little to benefit it. Louis-Philippe of Orléans, who reigned 1830–48, carried out renovation work which took its toll on the buildings.

During the late 19th and the 20th century Versailles' main function was as a military headquarters: for the Germans during the Franco-Prussian War, for the Allied War Council during World War I, and then in World War II, from 1944 to 1945, for the Allies.

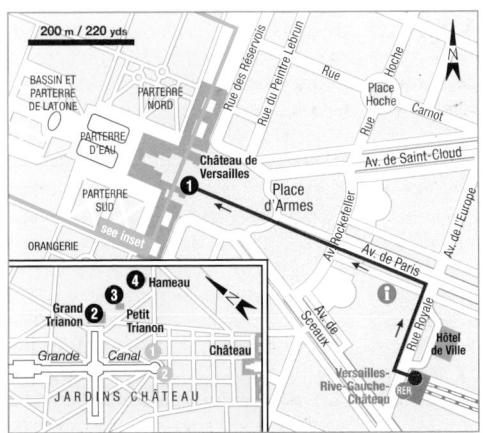

Palace ceiling

THE MAIN PALACE

Start the tour at the main palace, which can be visited without a guide. It includes the **Grands Appartements** (State Apartments) of the King and Queen, where the monarch's every move was scrutinised by a league of courtiers.

Here too is the **Galerie des Glaces** (Hall of Mirrors), best visited in the afternoon, when the sun streams in. Seventeen arched windows correspond to 17 mirrored arcades, and the vaulted ceiling features captions from the playwright Racine and 30 paintings by Lebrun of great events from the first 17 years of Louis XIV's 72-year reign. It was in this room that the Treaty of Versailles was signed to signify the end of World War I.

For a supplement, you can see Louis XIV's private bedroom and the apartments of the Dauphin and Dauphine. Guided tours are offered for the private apartments of Louis XV, Louis XVI, Marie Antoinette, Madame de Pompadour and Madame du Barry, as well as the opera house and royal chapel.

TRIANONS AND HAMEAU

The two other main buildings on the estate are the Grand and Petit Trianons, located to the northwest, about 30 minutes on foot from the château. If you do not want to walk, take the mini train that runs regularly from the château, along the Grand Canal and across to the Trianons and back. Marie-Antoinette's Hameau (classed, along with the Petit Trianon, as 'Marie-Antoinette's Estate') is a cluster of thatched cottages, a 10-minute walk to the northeast.

Grand Trianon

The Italianate **Grand Trianon** ❷ was erected by Louis XIV as a miniature palace and haven from public life in the main château. Le Vau's original design of 1670 was replaced in 1687 with the marble architecture of Hardouin-Mansart that you see today. After being looted during the Revolution, the Grand Trianon was later redecorated in the Empire style for Napoleon and his second wife Marie-Louise. In more recent times, Charles de

---

A public way of life

The Versailles complex was designed to house the entire court and its entourage: some 20,000 people. Leaving their provincial châteaux or Parisian mansions, members of the nobility were obliged to spend years in service at court, at great personal expense, observing an elaborate system of etiquette in order to try to win the king's favour. Instead of plotting civil war, nobles fought for the honour of holding the king's shirt when he got out of bed in the morning during the celebrated public levée. Similarly, the king's meals were public ceremonies, and queens even gave birth in full view of courtiers.

The King's State Bedroom

Gaulle stayed here during his presidency, and ever since, one wing has been reserved for the French Head of State.

Petit Trianon and Hameau
The **Petit Trianon** ❸ was built for Louis XV in the Greek style by Gabriel from 1762 to 1768 as a retreat for the king and his mistresses Madame de Pompadour, and later Madame du Barry. The gardens here were re-landscaped in the rambling English style for Marie Antoinette, who was given the Petit Trianon on her accession to the throne.

Also linked with Marie Antoinette is the **Hameau** ❹, a cluster of thatched cottages by architect Richard Mique. The official Versailles guidebooks stress that these rustic-style buildings were not erected, as is popularly believed, so that the Queen could play at being a shepherdess, but as a dairy where food for the royal estate was produced.

THE GARDENS AND PARK

The château's 815ha (2,000 acres) of gardens and park are the work of André Le Nôtre, who created the ultimate French playground for Louis XIV out of unpromising hillocks and marshland.

A principal feature of the park is the **Grand Canal**, an ornamental stretch of water covering 44ha (105 acres), which can be explored by boat. Around the canal, a network of pathways, fountain basins, groves adorned with statuary, and sculpted trees and bushes, radi-

ates out symmetrically. Look out for the **Orangerie**, with a vaulted gallery that could house over 2,000 orange trees, and the king's vegetable garden.

Fountain displays
Note that there is an extra charge for the gardens on Tuesdays, Saturdays and Sundays in season, when the fountains, powered by an ingenious hydraulic system, come to life and 17th-century music blasts over the *parterres*.

Eating
Of the cafés and restaurants within the grounds, two of the best are **La Flottille**, see ❶, and **La Petite Venise**, see ❷. There are also inexpensive open-air eating areas serving snacks in the groves on either side of the Latona Garden and Royal Avenue.

Food and Drink

❶ LA FLOTTILLE
Tel: 01 39 51 41 58; €€
At the head of the Grand Canal is this restaurant (serving standard French fare), brasserie and *salon de thé*.

❷ LA PETITE VENISE
Tel: 01 39 53 25 69; €€€
Located between the Bassin d'Apollon and the Grand Canal, this Italian restaurant has contemporary décor and wines from Sicily, Tuscany and Venice.

The stunning entrance to the château

FONTAINEBLEAU

Louis IX called Fontainebleau his 'wilderness', François I referred to trips here as 'coming home', and, from exile in St Helena, Napoleon Bonaparte called it 'the true home of kings'. Little wonder that, like Versailles, it is a World Heritage Site.

DISTANCE: 120km (74miles) rtn
TIME: A full day
START/END: Fontainebleau
POINTS TO NOTE: The distance above is from Paris. To reach the palace by train: from the Gare de Lyon to Fontainebleau-Avon (45 mins), then 'Château' bus from the station or 30-min walk through town. By car: take the Fontainebleau exit on the A6 autoroute; the château is 16km (10 miles) away. Parking is available in the town.

Close to the town centre of Fontaineb-leau is the **Château de Fontaineb-leau** ❶ (place Général-de-Gaulle; www. musee-chateau-fontainebleau.fr; Wed–Mon Oct–Mar 9.30am–5pm, Apr–Sept until 6pm; charge), the only fully furnished royal palace in France.

BACKGROUND

In 1528, to indulge his passion for blood sports, François I commissioned a palace in the Mannerist style on the site of a medi-eval royal hunting lodge near the Fôret de Fontainebleau. Back from his conquests in Italy, François introduced to France the Renaissance style, which became known as the First Fontainebleau School.

Palace evolution

Additions were carried out under Henri II, Henri IV, Louis XIV and Louis XVI, but with the latter came the French Revolution, and the palace was no longer the home of kings. It was stripped of its contents and left to ruin, until 1803, when Napoleon founded a military school here and began a full refurbishment. During the Bourbon Restoration (1815–30), Louis Philippe continued the renovation, followed, in the

Food and Drink

❶ **LE FRANÇOIS 1ER (CHEZ BERNARD)**
3 rue Royale, Fontainebleau; tel: 01 64 22 24 68; €€
This great restaurant has a terrace overlooking the château. Chef Bernard Crogiez's cuisine is especially fine in game season.

The Louis XVI wing

Second Republic, by Napoleon III. In the late 19th century Empress Eugénie added new salons and a Chinese Museum. From 1945–65 the palace was the headquarters of the military branch of NATO.

PALACE TOUR

The entrance is on the right-hand side of the **Cour du Cheval Blanc** (White Horse Courtyard), as you stand facing the double-horseshoe staircase. This is the Louis XV wing, which houses the **Musée Napoléon I**, showcasing clothing, weapons and paintings relating to the emperor.

First floor

At the end of this wing, ascend the stairs to the **Grands Appartements** (State Apartments) and Renaissance rooms. Highlights include the Galerie François I,

emblazoned with his initials and heraldic salamander, the ballroom and the Salon Louis XIII. Also exceptional is the Galerie de Diane and the king's bedroom, transformed in 1808 into a throne room, as well as Napoleon's elegant Imperial Apartment.

Ground floor

On the ground floor, to the left of the grand staircase, is the 16th-century **Chapelle de la Trinité**, in which Louis XV was married in 1725. Ahead are the modest **Petits Appartements** (Small Apartments; restricted hours), which Napoleon I created as a private suite.

You can also visit Empress Eugénie's salons and the **Musée Chinois** (Chinese Museum; restricted hours).

The garden

Highlights in the grounds include the early 19th-century English garden, the carp pond, the Grand Parterre, the canal and what is still the largest *jeu de paume* (real-tennis court) in the world.

BACK TO TOWN

After your visit, exit the main gate, cross place d'Armes and head along rue du Château (later rue Grande). Our recommendation of where to eat in town is the **François 1er**, see ❶.

Monet's house

GIVERNY

A visit to Monet's house, at Giverny in Normandy, is an exercise in retinal pleasure. Gardens brimming with flowers, a Japanese bridge, waterlilies and a pink house: it's easy to see why he proclaimed it 'a splendid spot for me'.

DISTANCE: 160km (100 miles) rtn
TIME: A full day
START: Fondation Monet
END: Musée des Impressionnismes
POINTS TO NOTE: To reach the start point by train: from the Gare St-Lazare to Vernon (45 mins) trains are infrequent, so check times in advance (www.sncf.fr); at Vernon take a bus 15 mins to the village (no. 241 leaves the station about 15 mins after the arrival of Paris train); or, rent a bike from opposite the station (E14 per day, 25 mins ride on the flat; see www.fondation-monet.com for details of the route). By car: take the A13 west to Bonnières, then the D201 to Giverny.

Claude Monet (1840–1926) discovered Giverny, where the Seine meets the river Epte, in 1883, spying it from the door of the little train that used to run at the bottom of what is now the Clos Normand garden. He moved here with his own two children, his mistress Alice Heschedé (his wife had died of tuberculosis in 1879) and her six children, and lived here for 43 years until his death.

In the early years, Monet was desperately short of money, and his art dealer, Durand-Ruel, helped him pay the rent. Eventually, though, the painter prospered: he purchased this house, married Alice, and laid out the gardens you see today at great expense.

FONDATION MONET

From the car and coach parks, it is just a hop to 84 rue Claude Monet and the **Fondation Monet ❶** (www.fondation-monet.fr; Apr–Oct daily 9.30am–6pm; charge). Beyond the ticket booth, you reach the museum shop, once one of the many studios that Monet built around the property, and used for the production of the waterlily paintings, *Les Nymphéas*, now in the Musée de l'Orangerie (see page 34) in Paris.

The house

After the shop, on the right, is Monet's eccentrically coloured house: pink and green on the outside, while inside the din-

His 'Japanese Bridge'

Waterlilies in the Water Garden

ing room is bright yellow, and the kitchen is sky blue. Upstairs are the bedrooms with big windows on to the gardens. The walls of the artist's rooms feature Japanese prints from his extensive collection.

Food and Drink

1 TERRA CAFÉ

99 rue Claude Monet, Giverny; tel: 02 32 51 94 61; 10am–6pm; €€

This restaurant offers salads, quiches, fish and grilled meat, and fine views of the pretty gardens from the terrace. You can eat here without a museum ticket.

2 HÔTEL BAUDY

81 rue Claude Monet, Giverny; tel: 02 32 21 10 03; daily 10am–11.30pm; €€

Once the focal point for the village's American artists, this hotel has a restaurant that does classic French food and terrace seating.

The garden

The garden is already familiar to many from Monet's paintings. In front of the house is the grid pattern of flowerbeds of the Clos Normand. Below is the Water Garden, for which Monet bought the land in 1893. Obtaining official permission to dig his ponds was a protracted business, but by 1895 Monet was able to have his waterlilies, the Japanese bridge, the willows and the pond with punt. In 1966, Monet's son Michel bequeathed the property to the state.

MUSÉE DES IMPRESSIONNISMES

After the gardens, turn left out of the Fondation and walk along rue Claude Monet. At no. 99 is the **Musée des Impressionnismes 2** (www.museedesimpressionnismesgiverny.com; Apr–Oct daily 10am–6pm; charge), devoted to American artists, who, inspired by the Movement, came to Giverny. You can lunch here at **Terra Café**, see 1, or further on the same road, see 2.

Monet was initially receptive to the arrivals, but tired of the invasion: 'When I first came to Giverny I was quite alone, the little village was unspoiled. Now, so many artists, students, flock here, I have often thought of moving away.' As you leave, you may feel some sympathy.

A warm welcome from Mickey

DISNEYLAND PARIS

If your children are tired of art museums, and unimpressed with another lunch of foie gras, then Disneyland Resort Paris may be in order. Here, they can enjoy all the latest fairground rides and as many burgers as they can eat.

> **DISTANCE:** 64km (40 miles) rtn
> **TIME:** At least a full day
> **START/END:** Disneyland
> **POINTS TO NOTE:** The distance above is from central Paris. Directions on how to get to the park are as follows: by public transport, catch the RER A from central Paris at Auber, Châtelet or Étoile to Disneyland Resort Paris; by car, take the A4 east of Paris to Marne-la-Vallée (exit 14), where there are signs to the resort and car parks.

Located on a 83-ha (205-acre) site at Marne-la-Vallée, east of Paris, **Disneyland Resort Paris** ❶ (opening times vary considerably: for bookings and information, see www.disneylandparis.com) covers an area one-fifth of the size of Paris. It welcomed 16 million visitors in 2012 – more than any other single attraction in Europe – 52 percent of whom were from France and 13 percent from Britain. Given the amount to see, families might consider spreading a visit over two days. The on-site hotels are costly, but staying on the spot means early access to the attractions. The park's official language is English, but French is widely spoken.

Homecoming

According to the Disney marketing machine, Disneyland Paris was something of a homecoming; Walt's family came from Isigny-sur-Mer in Normandy, and the name d'Isigny (from Isigny) became Disney in the US. But financial governmental incentives, not family history, were behind the final decision to bring Disney to Europe.

The complex has three parts: the main park, Walt Disney Studios (a self-contained park that offers a behind-the-scenes look at the history of animation, film and television) and the hotels and shops of Disney Village.

THE MAIN PARK

Disneyland's 'imagineers' have created five 'magic lands': **Fantasyland**, the most popular area for children, with boat trips, carousels and a hedge maze;

Disney Village

Buzz Lightyear and Woody join in the fun

Main Street USA, representing the early 1900s, with ragtime and Dixieland bands (though also featuring Cinderella's Castle); **Frontierland**, evoking the wild west; **Adventureland**, with characters such as Captain Hook; and the futuristic **Discoveryland**, which has a Space Mountain, and French-themed attractions, such as an underwater trip that pays homage to celebrated French sci-fi writer Jules Verne's *20,000 Leagues Under the Sea*.

WALT DISNEY STUDIOS

Disneyland Resort Paris celebrated its 10th anniversary in 2002 by opening up **Walt Disney Studios ❷**, which has four studio lots to entice visitors. Directly through the entrance is Front Lot, a mock film set of a street. There's also Production Courtyard, giving an insight into the production process; this will be the site of the Studio Tram Tour, a ride that will let you see what it feels like to be slap-bang in the middle of the filming action.

Then there's Backlot, which documents stunts and special effects – a great area for older children, teens and adults. And lastly there's Toon Studio, which goes back to basics with pen and paper to explain how animated classics are made.

DISNEY VILLAGE

The wider resort, **Disney Village**, is a celebration of 'Americana' and home to the resort hotels. Hotel Cheyenne is the most imaginative: a film-set Western hotel, with saloon, sheriff's jail and wooden-planked stores. Several hotels overlook Lake Disney, including Hotel New York, offering luxury rooms in a Manhattan-style skyscape.

The jewel in the park's crown is the elegant Victorian-style Disneyland Hotel, while in a forest 5km (3 miles) from the main park is Davy Crockett Ranch, where accommodation comprises camping and caravanning places and log cabins, with bike hire available.

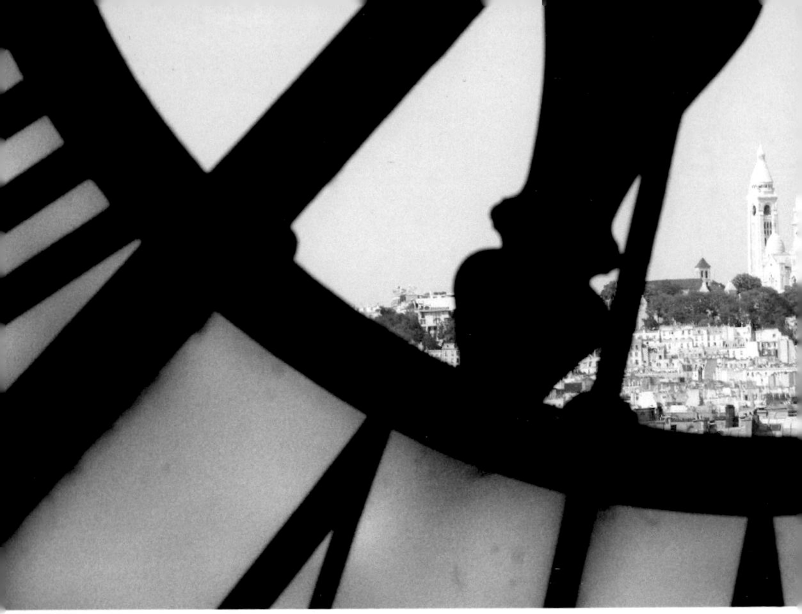

MAIGRET
FRANK PARRISH
La mouche
et l'araignée
5€
Victor Hugo
Notre-Dame
de Paris
Bergerac

13

CASSADES
CHOCOLAT
CAFÉ
LIÉGEOIS VIENNOIS

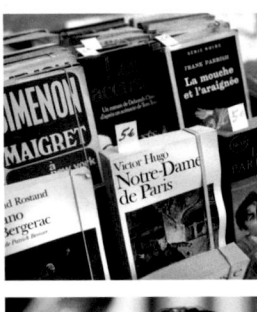

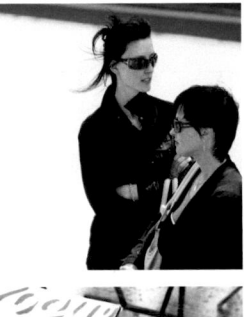

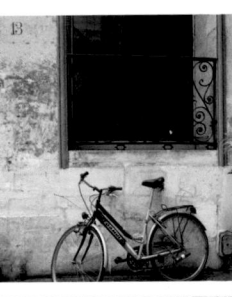

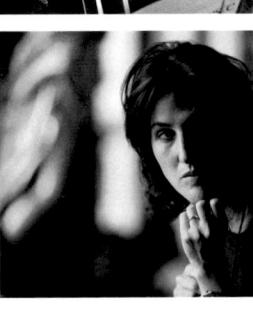

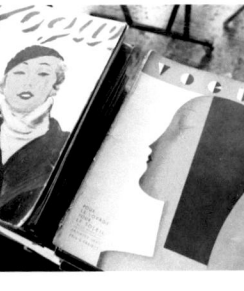

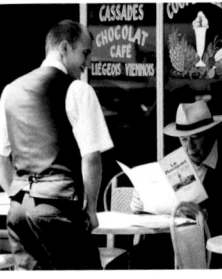

DIRECTORY

Hand-picked hotels and restaurants to suit all budgets and tastes, organised by area, plus select nightlife listings, an alphabetical listing of practical information, a language guide and an overview of the best books and films to give you a flavour of the city.

ACCOMMODATION

Paris has the second-largest number of hotel rooms in Europe (after London), with hotels ranging from the pint-sized to the palatial. Most hotels in the centre are concentrated in the 8th *arrondissement* (around the Champs-Élysées), the 9th (around the Opéra and Grand Magasins) and in the 10th (near the Gare du Nord). There are few hotels in the budget range – most are in the two- and three-star category. Don't expect to find a bargain – in general, it's hard to find anything really good, with its own bathroom, for less than 100 euros. In the middle range, the stress is generally on style and charm rather than high-tech facilities.

An alternative to staying in a hotel is a bed and breakfast. Several companies organise home stays. Alcôve & Agapes Bed & Breakfast à Paris (www.bed-and-breakfast-in-paris. com) has more than 100 homes on its register. Good Morning Paris (43 rue Lacépède, 5th; www.good morningparis.fr) offers rooms throughout the city (prices from €70 for one person to about €129 for three).

Hotel prices in Paris are not subject to restrictions and can be changed without notice, so check before booking. The majority of hotels vary prices by season. State your arrival time if you book by phone, or your room will not be held after 7pm.

Not all properties are wheelchair-accessible; even if a hotel does have an elevator, for example, it is likely that it will be a fairly small one. Travellers with disabilities should check before reserving.

The Islands

Hôtel des Deux-Iles

59 rue St-Louis-en-l'Ile, 4th; tel: 01 43 26 13 35; www.deuxiles-paris-hotel.com; metro: Pont Marie; €€€€
A peaceful and attractive hotel in a 17thcentury mansion house in the Ile St-Louis. Some rooms have views over a pretty courtyard.

Hôtel Henri IV

25 place Dauphine, 1st; tel: 01 43 54 44 53; www.henri4hotel.fr; metro: Pont Neuf; €
Some of the least expensive rooms in Paris can be found at this modest hotel which has been popular with visitors on a budget for decades. The 21 rooms are somewhat old-fashioned, with shared bathrooms, but this pales into insignificance beside the fabu-

> Price for a double room for one night without breakfast:
> €€€€= over 300 euros
> €€€ = 200–300 euros
> €€ = 100–200 euros
> € = below 100 euros

lous location on place Dauphine, only a short walk away from Notre-Dame and St-Michel. Reserve well in advance. Breakfast included.

Hôtel du Jeu de Paume

54 rue St-Louis-en-l'Ile, 4th; tel: 01 43 26 14 18; www.jeudepaumehotel.com; metro: Pont Marie; €€€–€€€€

Delightfully set on the pretty Île St-Louis, this hotel, with ancient beams, had a contemporary makeover in 2010 but still retains its charm. Breakfast is served in the mansion's 17th-century real-tennis court (hence the name). Bar, library, Wi-Fi access, concierge, room service until 10pm and an attractive courtyard garden.

Hôtel Lutèce

65 rue St-Louis-en-l'Ile, 4th; tel: 01 43 26 23 52; www.paris-hotel-lutece.com; metro: Pont Marie; €€€

The Lutèce has the same owners as the Hôtel des Deux-Iles, and is similarly charming, rich in 17th-century beams and stonework. The wood-panelled sitting room has a superb fireplace, and rooms are decorated in warm colours.

Louvre, Tuileries and Concorde

Hôtel Brighton

218 rue de Rivoli, 1st; tel: 01 47 03 61 61; www.esprit-de-france.com; metro: Tuileries; €€

Recently restored, this hotel has several rooms that overlook the Jardin des Tuileries, and a reception area awash with gilt, marble and glass chandeliers. Rooms are large and decorated with a mix of traditional quality fabrics, careful lighting and sober furniture and artworks. The rooms with the fine views are understandably popular, so book well ahead.

Hôtel Costes

239 rue St-Honoré, 1st; tel: 01 42 44 50 00; www.hotelcostes.com; metro: Tuileries; €€€€

This hip hotel is just off elegant place Vendôme in an exclusive neighbourhood lined with chic boutiques. The rooms are exquisitely decorated with Baroque paintings, heavy drapes and antiques. Some bathrooms have clawfoot bathtubs and mosaic tiles. The hallways are lit with candles; even the indoor pool, which has an underwater sound system, is dark. Other facilities include a bar, gym, restaurant, room service and parking.

Grand Hôtel du Palais Royal

4 rue de Valois, 1st; tel: 01 42 96 15 35 www.grandhoteldupalaisroyal.com; metro: Palais Royal; €€€€

In an 18th-century building in the south eastern corner of the elegant Palais Royal is this intimate luxury hotel, which opened its doors in the summer of 2013. The 68 rooms and suites, some with their own balcony, successfully marry classical style with contemporary lines; the Terrace Suite unsurprisingly

Intimate decor

has its own terrace with great views over the city. As well as a restaurant and bar, there's also a spa, which uses Carita products and has a Turkish bath, and a fitness centre.

Opéra and Grands Boulevards

Banke Hotel

20 rue La Fayette, 9th; tel: 01 55 33 22 22; www.derbyhotels.com; metro: Chaussée d'Antin – La Fayette, Gare St-Lazare; €€€

Located in the heart of the Grands Boulevards, in the imposing Haussmannian former headquarters of the Crédit Commercial de France (CCF) bank, this hotel screams luxury and comfort, right from the vast domed reception area. There are 94 soundproofed rooms, which are richly decorated in chocolates, purples, reds and creams, reminiscent of a gentleman's club, with highlights of gold; those on the 6th floor have views of the Sacré-Cœur and the Palais-Garnier. Facilities include several restaurants (including the Josefin, which offers Spanish dishes), a bar, gym and spa. There's even a private art collection.

Hôtel Chopin

10 boulevard Montmartre (46 passage Jouffroy), 9th; tel: 01 47 70 58 10; www.hotelchopin.fr; metro: Richelieu Drouot; €

Tucked away at the end of an historic 19th-century glass-and-steel-roofed arc-ade, this is a quiet, friendly and simply furnished hotel, offering 36 rooms at a fabulous price for the location. Facilities are basic, but there are televisions in the rooms, and they are en suite. Book well in advance.

Hôtel Langlois

63 rue St-Lazare, 9th; tel: 01 48 74 78 24; www.hotel-langlois.com; metro: Trinité; €€

If you fancy stepping back in time then this three-star hotel is the place for you. Rooms are decorated in Belle Epoque and Art Nouveau style, each furnished with individual antiques and paintings, each with original features dating from 1870 when the building was constructed. The continental breakfast isn't cheap (€13) but it's worth trying just to check out the old-fashioned birdcage in the breakfast room. A taste of Paris from days gone by.

Hôtel Mansart

5 rue des Capucines, 1st; tel: 01 42 61 50 28; www.esprit-de-france.com; metro: Madeleine, Opéra; €€

Named in honour of Jules Hardouin-Mansart, architect to Louis XIV, and good value for this location, just off über-chic place Vendôme. The lobby has abstract murals inspired by designs for French formal gardens, and the spacious, high-ceilinged rooms are furnished with antiques and oil paintings: the duplex Vendôme suite looks out over the square itself.

Ready for bed   *The five-star Plaza Athénée*

Hôtel Plaza Athénée

25 avenue Montaigne, 8th; tel: 01 53 67 66 65; www.plaza-athenee-paris.com; metro: Alma Marceau; €€€€

This palatial hotel, with lavish mostly Louis XVI- or Regency-style decor, has sound-proofed rooms, a club, gym, 'Dior Institut' spa and an eponymous restaurant headed by super-chef Alain Ducasse. If you can't stretch to the price of a room, treat yourself to a cocktail in the fashionable bar.

Marais

Hôtel de la Bretonnerie

22 rue St-Croix-de-la-Bretonnerie, 4th; tel: 01 48 87 77 63; www.bretonnerie.com; metro: St-Paul, Hôtel de Ville; €€

Historic features abound in this delightful Marais hotel set in a 17th-century *hôtel particulier*. The rooms and seven suites are all furnished with lavish fabrics and rich colours; some have wooden beams and romantic four-poster beds.

Hôtel Caron de Beaumarchais

12 rue du Vieille du Temple, 4th; tel: 01 42 72 34 12; www.carondebeaumarchais.com; metro: St-Paul, Hôtel de Ville; €€

A gorgeous little hotel in an excellent location in one of the nicest streets in the Marais. Rooms are decorated in the romantic French 18th-century style with pretty chandeliers and antiques, in honour of the 18th-century playwright after whom the hotel is named. Very friendly management. There are only 19 rooms, so book in advance.

Hôtel Duo

11 rue du Temple, 4th; tel: 01 42 72 72 22; www.duoparis.com; metro: Hôtel de Ville; €€€

Trendy hotel in a great spot in the Marais, just steps from the Hôtel de Ville. The 58 rooms, which are quiet despite the central location, thanks to excellent sound-proofing, are furnished in contemporary style, with good-sized bathrooms (unusual in Paris). Facilities include a bar, gym, sauna and Wi-Fi internet access.

Hôtel Jules & Jim

11 rue des Gravilliers, 3rd; tel: 01 44 54 13 13; www.hoteljulesetjim.com; metro: Arts et Métiers; €€€

Opened in 2011, this super-cool, gay-friendly hotel pays homage to François Truffaut's famous film of the same name. The 23 stylish-yet-simple rooms (think wood, glass and stone) are based in three buildings around two courtyards.

Pavillon de la Reine

28 place des Vosges, 3rd; tel: 01 40 29 19 19; www.pavillon-de-la-reine.com; metro: St Paul; €€€€

This romantic mid-sized hotel, located on the elegant place des Vosges, feels like a chic country château. Rooms vary greatly in size and price, but

View from the top of Terrass in Montmartre

most have four-poster beds, exposed wooden beams and antiques. There's also a cosy lobby bar with evening wine tasting, and manicured gardens, plus the Spa de la Reine, with fitness room, jacuzzi, treatment booths and steam room.

Hôtel du Petit Moulin

29 rue du Poitou, 3rd; tel: 01 42 74 10 10; www.hoteldupetitmoulin.com; metro: St-Sébastien Froissart, Filles du Calvaire; €€
This fashionable hotel in the Marais was designed by Christian Lacroix using sumptuous fabrics and screen-printed *trompe l'œil* to create comfort and individuality. The reception occupies an old bakery, still with its painted glass ceiling panels, while the bar marries zinc counter, murals and pop colours.

Hôtel de la Place des Vosges

12 rue de Birague, 4th; tel: 01 42 72 60 46; www.hotelplacedesvosges.com; metro: St Paul; €–€€
An intimate hotel with only 16 rooms in a former stables. It's popular and in a great location by the place des Vosges, so book ahead. A successful marriage of old and new, although still slightly crumbly. Friendly staff.

Champs-Élysées, Trocadéro and West

Hôtel Daniel

8 rue Frédéric Bastiat, 8th; tel: 01 42 56 17 00; www.hoteldanielparis.com; metro: St-Philippe du-Roule, Franklin D. Roosevelt; €€€€
A member of the prestigious Relais & Châteaux group, the upmarket Hôtel Daniel is wonderfully romantic, with rooms exquisitely decorated with chinoiserie wallpaper, plush carpets and pretty antiques. Facilities include a bar, restaurant, Wi-Fi internet access, parking and room service. An excellent location for the Champs-Élysées and rue du Faubourg StHonoré.

Four Seasons George V

31 avenue George V, 8th; tel: 01 49 52 70 00; www.fourseasons.com/paris; metro: George V, Alma Marceau; €€€€
One of the most famous hotels in Paris, just off the Champs-Élysées. The George V offers the height of opulence, with beautifully decorated, traditional-style rooms with modern touches and magnificent marble bathrooms. Facilities include a fabulous spa inspired by the palace at Versailles, a bar, two restaurants, including the Michelin-starred Le Cinq, and a business centre. Exquisite service.

La Maison

8 rue Jean Goujon, 8th; tel: 01 40 74 64 65; www.lamaisonchampselysee.com; metro: Champs-Elysées-Clémenceau; €€€€
Ultra-stylish 40-room hotel in a Haussmannian building with minimalist interior decoration by fashion designer Martin Margiela. Enjoy a cocktail in 'The

Haussmannian–style apartments

Blind Bar', light up in 'The Cigar Bar' or savour a copious brunch on Sundays. There is a restaurant with a nice outside terrace too.

Hôtel de Sers

41 avenue Pierre 1er de Serbie, 8th; tel: 01 53 23 75 75; www.hoteldesers.com; metro: Alma Marceau; €€€€

The Sers combines modern style and comfort with the classic service of a traditional small French hotel. It has brushed-concrete floors downstairs, an interior courtyard with perpetually changing coloured light washes, modern furniture and very sleek bathrooms. But young architect Thomas Vidalenc has cleverly warmed up the minimalism with lots of lilac and crimson in carpets and curtains, as well as a witty nod to its Belle Epoque origins in the gallery of portraits in the hallway.

Le Sezz

6 avenue Frémiet, 16th; tel: 01 56 75 26 26; www.hotelsezz-paris.com; metro: Passy; €€€€

Le Sezz opened for business in 2005: behind its antique facade it's a seriously glam boutique hotel designed by hot furniture designer Christophe Pillet, which means one-way mirrored partitions between bedrooms and bathrooms, oversized soaking tubs, large shaggy rugs in red or green, dark concrete-like walls and a plethora of straight lines.

Hôtel de la Trémoille

14 rue de la Trémoille, 8th; tel: 01 56 52 14 00; www.hotel-tremoille.com; metro: Alma Marceau; €€€€

This discreetly elegant hotel has been thoroughly modernised yet retains its sense of Parisian style – 19th-century panelling, mouldings and fireplaces meet contemporary lighting and fabrics, and the comforts of air conditioning, internet access and so on. There's a fitness room and spa facilities in the basement. It's a calm hideaway, and you can even have your breakfast dispatched to you in privacy through a hatch by the door. Attached is the similarly elegant Le Louis bar and restaurant.

Montmartre

Hôtel Amour

8 rue Navarin, 9th; tel: 01 48 78 31 80; www.hotelamourparis.fr; metro: St-Georges; €€–€€€

Trendy boutique hotel in the style of an exclusive English gentleman's club, with 20 rooms decorated by contemporary artists; some of them even feature art installations. The bar has DJs, and the pretty restaurant has a garden out the back.

Hôtel Particulier

23 avenue Junot, 18th; tel: 01 53 41 81 40; www.hotel-particulier-montmartre.com; metro: Lamarck-Caulaincourt; €€€€

Gorgeous small hotel in a townhouse on one of the most desirable streets in Paris. The five suites are individually

decorated with antiques, design classics and sumptuous fabrics. Dinner, by reservation only, is available Wednesday to Sunday. A great place to get away from it all.

Hôtel Royal Fromentin

11 rue Fromentin, 9th; tel: 01 48 74 85 93; www.hotelroyalfromentin.com; metro: Blanche; €€

A hotel not far from Pigalle with its own special touches typical of the neighbourhood: the lobby was formerly a cabaret dating from the 1930s, the Dom Juan, and it still has the original wood panelling and some appropriate cabaret paraphernalia. Several of its 47 rooms have views of the Sacré-Cœur; the decor is bright but fairly traditional, and rooms are spacious and clean. There's a vintage glass lift, too.

Terrass

12–14 rue Joseph-Maistre, 18th; tel: 01 46 06 72 85; www.terrass-hotel.com; metro: Abbesses; €€€

The main attraction of this Montmartre hotel is the view from the rooftop restaurant – it is superb, taking in the whole of Paris. It's a favourite with some celebrities, who favour the hotel's plush suites. The rest of the rooms are comfortable if unremarkable. Cosy bar area with a roaring fire in winter months.

The East and Northeast

Hôtel Beaumarchais

3 rue Oberkampf, 11th; tel: 01 53 36 86 86; www.hotelbeaumarchais.com; metro: Filles du Calvaire; €

A fun, good-value designer hotel located in the trendy Oberkampf district, with plenty of nightlife nearby. The 31 rooms are painted in bright, primary colours. There's a terrace for breakfast in summer, and private parking (for a separate charge).

Hôtel Garden St Martin

35 rue Yves-Toudic, 10th; tel: 01 42 40 17 72; metro: Jacques Bonsergent; €€

Situated near the Canal St-Martin, a little off the beaten track, this is a value-for-money hotel with a small garden terrace and an even smaller lift. All the rooms are clean and compact.

Le Général

5–7 rue Rampon, 11th; tel: 01 47 00 41 57; www.legeneralhotel.com; metro: République; €€€

This hotel, a stone's throw from République, offers the boutique experience at reasonable(ish) prices. The rooms are beautifully decorated, minimalist yet cosy. There's a gym, a sauna and a bar. Room service is available 24/7, and there's Wi-Fi internet access too.

Mama Shelter

109 rue de Bagnolet, 20th; tel: 01 43 48 48 48; www.mamashelter.com; metro: Gambetta, Porte de Bagnolet; €–€€€

Located slightly off the beaten track, just east of Père-Lachaise cemetery, this Philippe Starck-designed hotel is

Eastern Paris offers more budget options than elsewhere in Paris

billed as a 'sensual refuge'. It is large (172 rooms) and industrial in style, but the biggest surprise is the price, with rooms from around 80 euros, meaning that you really can get design on a budget. Rooms are stylish and contemporary with their own entertainment systems. As well as hosting DJ sets at weekends, facilities include a restaurant, a pizzeria, two chic bars and a shop selling such indispensable items as toothbrushes and phone chargers. Genius.

Hôtel Original

8 boulevard Beaumarchais, 11th; tel: 01 47 00 91 50; www.hoteloriginalparis.com; metro: Bastille; €€€

The latest offering from fashion designer Stella Cadente is in a great location between places des Vosges and place de la Bastille. The 30 rooms in this ultra-modern boutique hotel have been individually and colourfully decorated and possess all mod cons including an iHome docking station, a plasma TV and free Wi-Fi.

Le Pavillon Bastille

65 rue de Lyon, 12th; tel: 01 43 43 65 65; www.paris-hotel-pavillonbastille.com; metro: Bastille; €€

Classy, contemporary hotel situated behind an attractive courtyard opposite the Opéra Bastille. Decor is modern and well kept, and facilities and services such as Wi-Fi are excellent. Popular with business people.

Hôtel Saint-Louis Bastille

114 boulevard Richard-Lenoir, 11th; tel: 01 43 38 29 29; www.saintlouisbastille.com; metro: Oberkampf; €€

Recently renovated, this affordable hotel is a perfect base for the dedicated bar-hopper, as it's on the corner of rue Oberkampf, still one of the liveliest nightlife hubs in the city. Five of the 27 rooms are singles; the decor is unremarkable, but rooms do have air conditioning and Wi-Fi; breakfast is served in a vaulted basement.

The Latin Quarter and St-Germain

Abbaye St-Germain

10 rue Cassette, 6th; tel: 01 45 44 38 11; www.hotelabbayeparis.com; metro: St-Sulpice; €€€–€€€€

This 17th-century abbey is excellently situated between the Jardin du Luxembourg and St-Germain-des-Prés, and has been sensitively converted into a hotel. The old-style decor, such as the beams and wood panelling, is charming, but there are all modern conveniences, too. Breakfast is served in the garden in summer by attentive staff. Facilities include Wi-Fi internet access, room service and a bar.

Hôtel d'Angleterre

44 rue Jacob, 6th; tel: 01 42 60 34 72; www.hotel-dangleterre.com; metro: St-Germain, Rue du Bac; €€€

This delightful hotel was the site on which the Treaty of Paris, proclaiming

the independence of the US, was prepared in 1783; during the 19th century it was used as the British Embassy. Ernest Hemingway lodged here (in room 14) in 1921. The rooms are fairly small and furnished with antiques; only the top-floor doubles are spacious. There's a lovely terrace and garden, where breakfast is served in summer.

Le Clos Médicis

56 rue Monsieur-le-Prince, 6th; tel: 01 43 29 10 80; www.closmedicis.com; metro: Cluny-Sorbonne, RER Luxembourg; €€

This stylish boutique hotel in an 18th-century *hôtel particulier* near the Jardin du Luxembourg offers chic bedrooms, antique tiles in the bathrooms, fabulous flower arrangements, an open fire in the lounge in winter and helpful staff. There's also a courtyard garden.

Hôtel Les Degrés de Notre Dame

10 rue des Grands-Degrés, 5th; tel: 01 55 42 88 88; http://lesdegreshotel.monsite-orange.fr; metro: St-Michel; €€

Romantically furnished hotel in a fabulous location overlooking Notre-Dame (rooms 47 and 501 have views of the cathedral). The 10 rooms are exquisitely decorated with pretty antiques; original wooden beams add to the character. Book well in advance.

Hôtel Esmeralda

4 rue St-Julien-le-Pauvre, 5th; tel: 01 43 54 19 20; metro: St-Michel, Maubert Mutualité; €

The 17th-century Esmeralda, the ultimate in shabby chic, is one of those places you either love or loathe. Its 19 rooms have loud floral wallpaper (probably peeling off the walls), antique furniture (some say 'flea-ridden') and a rickety old staircase (no elevator) that takes some negotiating with suitcases. In addition to the extremely low prices (rooms from around 40 euros for a single) and the undeniable character, the attraction is the incredible location; just under half of the rooms have views of Notre-Dame directly across the Seine.

Hôtel de Nesle

7 rue de Nesle, 6th; tel: 01 43 54 62 41; www.hoteldenesleparis.com; metro: Odéon; €

A laid-back student and backpackers' hotel. Facilities are basic, but the 20 rooms (nine are en suite) are cheerfully decorated with murals, furnished according to eclectic themes and spotless. There is a garden with a pond, and a hammam.

Hôtel Le Six

14 rue Stanislas, 6th; tel: 01 42 22 00 75; www.hotel-le-six.com; metro: Vavin or Notre-Dame-des-Champs; €€€

Design-conscious but child-friendly boutique hotel where the rooms have iPod/iPhone docks, Nespresso machines and L'Occitane toiletries. Relax after a hard day's sightseeing with a drink in the glass-roofed lounge, book a private yoga class in the fitness centre or ease

Parisian hotels range from the pint-sized to the palatial

away aches and pains in the hammam. There's no restaurant but there is room service.

The 7th

Hôtel Lenox

9 rue de l'Université, 7th; tel: 01 42 96 10 95; www.hotelparislenoxsaintgermain. com; metro: St-Germain-des-Prés; €€–€€€

This trendy hotel on a quiet road in the up-market 7th arrondissement is decorated in classic modern style and is very popular among style-conscious creative types. The 34 recently renovated rooms are spotless, in warm chocolate and raspberry tones. Amenities include a bar, room service and Wi-Fi internet.

Hôtel de Verneuil

8 rue de Verneuil, 7th; tel: 01 42 60 82 14; www.hotel-verneuil-saint-germain.com; metro: St-Germain; €€–€€€

A cosy characterful hotel in an elegant 17th-century building in the up-market 7th arrondissement with small but attractive rooms, which recently had a modern makeover. Singer Serge Gainsbourg lived just opposite, and the wall outside his old house is decorated with graffiti in homage. Well placed for St-Germain. The hotel also has a smart apartment nearby.

Le Walt

37 avenue de La Motte-Picquet, 7th; tel: 01 45 51 55 83; www.lewaltparis.com; metro: Ecole Militaire; €€€€

This boutique hotel certainly has the glam factor: 25 rooms decorated in classic or contemporary style – some of which have views of the Eiffel Tower, and all of which have sleek glass-and-chrome bathrooms and large oil paintings over the bed – combine with wooden floors and a stylish little courtyard restaurant.

Montparnasse

Hôtel Aviatic

105 rue de Vaugirard, 6th; tel: 01 53 63 25 50; www.aviatic.fr; metro: Montparnasse-Bienvenüe; €€€

A little winter garden and a characterful lounge and reception area set the tone at this carefully put-together establishment. The breakfast room looks more like an old-fashioned bistro than part of a hotel, and rooms are decorated with objects picked up at flea markets. Book online to get the best deals.

La Maison Montparnasse

53 rue de Gergovie, 14th; tel: 01 45 42 11 39; www.lamaisonmontparnasse.com; metro: Pernety; €€

The owners of this lovely hotel, which opened in 2009, are keen that guests should feel at home, hence the name. Take your pick from 36 contemporary rooms where pink, yellow, purple or orange are the dominant colour schemes. Breakfast can be taken on the terrace in summer.

Champagne, the perfect apéritif

RESTAURANTS

France's dedication to the gastronomic arts is legendary, and the respect for food in all its forms is still strongly in evidence in the capital. Granted, it may not be as cheap as it once was to dine out here – even the classic set menus can seem pricey these days – but that doesn't seem to have deterred either Parisians or tourists. The city is peppered with great eateries, from bistros, brasseries and glitzy Michelin-starred restaurants to Breton crêperies and Moroccan couscousseries and top-notch Asian restaurants, all of which affords plenty of opportunity to sample life as a true *bon viveur*. Note that in up-market restaurants there is often a dress code, with a jacket requested and tie preferred for men. Note, too, that many restaurants close on Sunday evening (brasseries are the useful exception to this) and for the whole of August.

The Islands

Le Sergent Recruteur

41 rue St-Louis-en-l'Île, 4th; tel: 01 43 54 75 42; closed Sun–Mon; metro: Pont Marie; €€€€

Price guide for dinner for one with half a bottle of house wine:
€€€€€ = over 60 euros
€€€ = 40–60 euros
€€ = 25–40 euros
€ = under 25 euros

Stylish and fashionable new restaurant in ancient surroundings where chef Antonin Bonnet puts a contemporary twist on French market cuisine.

Le Tastevin

46 rue St-Louis-en-l'Ile, 4th; tel: 01 43 54 17 31; www.letastevin-paris.com; closed Mon lunch; metro: Pont-Marie; €€€

In a building dating from 1620 with a wood-panelled dining room, this gourmet restaurant has oodles of charm. Food is traditional French: try the crayfish salad for starters, then steak flambéed with thyme, followed by profiteroles or melt-in-the-middle chocolate pudding.

Louvre, Tuileries and Concorde

La Dame de Pic

20 rue du Louvre, 1st; tel: 01 42 60 40 40; www.ladamedepic.fr; closed Sun and Aug; metro: Louvre-Rivoli; €€€€

Opened in 2012, this is the first Paris restaurant of Anne-Sophie Pic, the only female French chef with three Michelin stars. A big fan of aromas and Japanese cuisine, the lunch menu (€49) includes chicken confit with turnip, date and Voatsiperifery pepper followed by pineapple with camomile and ginger. A sensual experience.

Le Grand Véfour

17 rue de Beaujolais, 1st; tel: 01 42 96 56

Leave space for dessert

Expect haute cuisine at Le Grand Véfour

27; www.grand-vefour.com; closed Sat–Sun and Aug; metro: Palais-Royal; €€€€

Hiding under the arches of the Palais-Royal is one of the most beautiful restaurants in Paris. Le Grand Véfour opened its doors in 1784 and has fed the likes of Emperor Napoleon and writers Alphonse Lamartine, Colette, and Victor Hugo. Today it serves haute cuisine under the aegis of chef Guy Martin.

Opéra and Grands Boulevards

Aux Lyonnais

32 rue St-Marc, 2nd; tel: 01 42 96 65 04; www.auxlyonnais.com; closed Sat lunch, Sun, Mon and Aug; metro: Grands Boulevards; €€€

Founded in 1892, this bistro still retains its original decor but has been beautifully revamped under top chef Alain Ducasse. The menu pays tribute to Lyonnaise specialities, with renditions of pike, perch and crayfish quenelles. Also highlights include frogs' legs, charcuterie, excellent cuts of beef and regional wines.

Chartier

7 rue du Faubourg Montmartre, 9th; tel: 01 47 70 86 29; www.bouillon-chartier.com; daily 11.30am–10pm; metro: Grands Boulevards; €

Chartier is the best-known low-price eatery in town. The atmosphere is an experience in itself, with Belle Epoque decor and snappy waiters, although there was some controversy a few years ago about the replacement of the checked tablecloths with white paper

ones. Expect shared tables and plenty of bonhomie. Arrive early if you want to stand a chance of getting a seat.

Gallopin

40 rue Notre-Dame-desVictoires, 2nd; tel: 01 42 36 45 38; www.brasseriegallopin.com; daily noon–1am; metro: Bourse; €€€

This brasserie opposite the Stock Exchange opened in 1876 and is still decorated in Belle Epoque style. The chef prepares refined versions of traditional dishes, including *pâté maison*, *steak tartare* and flambéed crêpes. The fish is a star attraction, with specialities such as haddock poached in milk with spinach, and delicious seafood platters. Excellent food in a distinguished setting.

Le Grand Colbert

2 rue Vivienne, 2nd; tel: 01 42 86 87 88; www.legrandcolbert.fr; daily noon–1am; metro: Bourse; €€€

This large, beautiful brasserie, which opened in 1830, offers the sort of traditional dishes that the French have always demanded from their brasseries. Choose from beef carpaccio, goat's cheese in pastry, sole meunière, Burgundian snails or frogs' legs in garlic, ripe cheeses, and creamy chocolate mousse and feathery light *îles flottantes* (soft meringues in custard).

Taillevent

15 rue Lamennais, 8th; tel: 01 44 95 15 01; www.taillevent.com; closed Sat, Sun and Aug; metro: George V; €€€€

Cafés are great for people watching

One of the most illustrious haute cuisine restaurants in Paris, but still surprisingly unstuffy. The food is magnificent: the earthy signature, spelt, is cooked 'like risotto' with bone marrow, black truffle, whipped cream and parmesan and is truly heavenly. Jacket requested.

The 7th

L'Arpège

84 rue de Varenne, 7th; tel: 01 47 05 09 06; Mon–Fri; metro: Varenne; €€€€
Chef Alain Passard has been called 'the poet of *terroir*' for his imaginative menus and signature dessert of tomato *confite* with 12 seasonings (if you can name them, the dish is free).

L'Atelier de Joël Robuchon

5 rue de Montalembert, 7th; tel: 01 42 22 56 56; lunch and dinner daily; metro: Rue du Bac, St-Germain-des-Prés; €€€€
Even jaded Parisians queue up in all weathers to sample the warm *foie gras* brochettes or tapenade with fresh tuna conjured up by one of France's most revered chefs. The restaurant is built around an open kitchen, so you can watch the masters at work, and the atmosphere is slick, like that of a bar. Reservations are advisable for sittings at 11.30am, noon, 12.30pm, 2pm, 2.30pm, 3.30pm and 6.30pm.

Au bon Accueil

14 rue de Monttessuy, 7th; tel: 01 47 05 46 11; Mon–Fri; metro: Ecole Militaire; €€€
The decor here is sophisticated and ele-gant, with a lightness of touch; likewise the cooking. The *prix-fixe* dinner menu (around €30) is exceptional value. Sit on the terrace for views of the Eiffel Tower.

Le Florimond

19 avenue de la Motte-Picquet, 7th; tel: 01 45 55 40 38; closed Sat lunch, Sun, Mon lunch and 1st Sat of the month; metro: Ecole Militaire, Latour Maubourg; €€–€€€
Pascal Guillaumin's bistro has a cosy, intimate atmosphere. His traditional French dishes are beautifully presented, and the service is warm and friendly. There's a great-value three-course set menu at lunch time for around €22; the evening set menu is €35.

Il Vino di Enrico Bernardo

13 boulevard de la Tour Maubourg, 7th; tel: 01 44 11 72 00; www.ilvinobyenrico bernardo.com; Mon–Sat dinner only; metro: Tour Maubourg, Invalides; €€€€
Milanese Enrico Bernardo turns the tra-ditional dining tables upside down at his restaurant where the food plays second fiddle to the wine. Diners choose their wines and then learn what dishes are on offer to complement them – or else go the whole hog on a full blind-tasting menu. It seems gimmicky but it works.

Le Voltaire

27 quai Voltaire, 7th; tel: 01 42 61 17 49; Tue–Sat; metro: Rue du Bac; €€€€
The food at this riverside bistro runs the whole gamut from rustic (such as sau-téed rabbit) to luxury (lobster omelette).

Paris is famous for its elaborate desserts

Champs-Élysées and Trocadéro

Alain Ducasse au Plaza Athénée

25 avenue Montaigne, 8th; tel: 01 53 67 65 00; www.alain-ducasse.com; lunch Thu–Fri, dinner Mon–Fri, closed last two weeks in Dec and mid-July to mid-Aug; metro: Alma-Marceau; €€€€

Cooking elevated to an art form from globetrotting chef Alain Ducasse, France's first recipient of six Michelin stars (three apiece for two restaurants), with the help of his acolyte Christophe Moret. According to Ducasse, his meals are not about fancy presentation but purity and essence of flavour. Expect truffles in abundance but also superb vegetables from Provence, where he first made his name. Jackets essential for men; tie recommended.

Les Bistronomes

34 rue de Richelieu, 1st; tel: 01 42 60 59 66; closed Sat lunch, Sun and Mon; metro: Quatre Septembre; €€€

It only opened in 2011 but this fashionable address was voted the best bistro in Paris in 2012. The menu consists of traditional French dishes, often with an update – try tempura of sardines with a tandoori tartar sauce followed by dark chocolate tart with blood orange jelly and ice cream.

Bistrot de la Poste

54 rue de Longchamp, 16th; tel: 01 47 55 01 31; closed Sat; metro: Trocadéro; €€€

In a nice location, this pleasant, comfortable bistrot serves well-executed classic French dishes. Sunday brunch (11am–4pm).

Galeries Lafayette

48 boulevard Haussmann, 9th; tel: 01 40 23 52 67; Mon–Sat 8.30am–9.30pm; metro: Chaussée d'Antin, RER Auber; €–€€

A good choice of restaurants and cafes under one roof, including French, Italian and Japanese, as well as branches of Pierre Hermé and Angelina which are both noted for their delicious cakes.

Minipalais

Avenue Winston Churchill, 8th; tel: 01 42 56 42 42; daily 10am–2am; metro: Champs-Elysées-Clémenceau; €€€

In the majestic surroundings of the Grand Palais, in a high-ceilinged room decorated with contemporary furniture, are served traditional dishes with a modern twist created by acclaimed chef Eric Frechon: try the duck *foie gras* burger drizzled with truffle *jus* followed by a simple strawberry and apple salad. The terrace, under a magnificent colonnade, is a delight on sunny days. A good place for just a drink too.

Le Pré Catelan

Route de Suresnes, Bois de Boulogne, 16th; tel: 01 44 14 41 14; closed Sun, Mon, two weeks in March, three weeks in Aug and last week in Oct; metro: Porte Maillot; €€€€

In the heart of the Bois de Boulogne, this is one of the most romantic spots in Paris. Frédéric Anton prepares spectacular

Food–obsessed Rue Montorgueil

haute cuisine centring on fresh truffles, lobster, lamb and fresh seafood. Reserve in advance.

Le Roi du Pot-au-feu

34 rue Vignon, 9th; tel: 01 47 42 37 10; closed Sun and mid-July–mid-Aug; metro: Madeleine; €

Traditional bistro (think red-and-white checked tablecloths) specialising in *pot-au-feu*. Once a rural stew eaten by peasant farmers, it is now a fashionable dish among Parisian gourmets. The best part is the bone marrow. Other French classics are also well executed here.

Stella Maris

4 rue Arsène Houssaye, 8th; tel: 01 42 89 16 22; closed Sat lunch and Sun; metro: George V; €€€€

Gourmet French cuisine à la Escoffier by Japanese chef Tateru Yoshino. Try tuna *tartare* with avocado and wasabi cream to start, followed by braised beef cheek, then Kouign Aman (Breton cake) with cider sorbet for dessert. Unstuffy modern dining room.

La Table Lauriston

129 rue Lauriston, 16th; tel: 01 47 27 00 07; closed Sat lunch, Sun and Aug; metro: Trocadéro; €€€

A bright, modern award-winning bistrot with traditional French cuisine such as terrine of pigs' trotters, frogs' legs in parsley sauce and lemon tart. The lunch menu is good value (around €30 for

three courses) and there is an extensive wine list, with the emphasis on smaller producers.

Beaubourg and Les Halles

Au Pied de Cochon

6 rue Coquillière, 1st; tel: 01 53 23 08 00; €€€

In its heyday, this all-night brasserie catered for market workers; now it is rather more upmarket. Still, the house speciality remains the same: grilled pig's trotter with Béarnaise sauce. Other star turns include the oysters and the onion soup (good for hangovers).

Benoît

20 rue St-Martin, 4th; tel: 01 42 72 25 76; www.benoit-paris.com; lunch and dinner daily, closed Aug; metro: Hôtel de Ville, Châtelet; €€€€

At this vintage bistro, renowned for its excellent cooking and high prices, master chef Alain Ducasse offers timeless terrines and casseroles. Highly professional service. A very chic affair.

La Fresque

100 rue Rambuteau, 1st; tel: 01 42 33 17 56; lunch and dinner daily; metro: Les Halles; €–€€

Sitting elbow to elbow at one of the big wooden tables is part of the charm here, as is the decor (white faïence tiles, frescoes, etc). The bistro fare, such as beef stew and duck, is excellent, and the staff are friendly. Always one vegetarian main course.

Simple but elegant soup

Al fresco lunch

Le Petit Marcel

65 rue Rambuteau, 4th; tel: 01 48 87 10 20;
cash only; metro: Rambuteau; €€

Inside, the walls are lined with Art Nouveau tiles and the ceiling is painted; outside, there is seating on the terrace. The menu comprises standard French fare – salads, steak frites, omelettes, tarts – but all well prepared, inexpensive and tasty.

Spring

6 rue Bailleul, 1st; tel: 01 45 96 05 72; lunch
Wed–Fri, dinner Tue–Sat; metro: Louvre-Rivoli; €€€€

Fashionable address where the guests eat what the American chef decides to cook (no menus). Around the corner, Spring Boutique (52 rue de l'Arbre Sec, Tue–Sat) is a more affordable lunch stop serving bowls of hearty chicken soup.

Marais and Bastille

404

69 rue des Gravilliers, 3rd; tel: 01 42 74
57 81; www.404-resto.com; lunch and
dinner daily, Sat–Sun brunch; metro: Arts et
Métiers; €€

Packed, hip and atmospheric, with low seating and iron grilles on the windows casting lacy patterns through the dim interior on to the tables. The Moroccan menu features filo-pastry pies, lamb brochettes, an exotic selection of couscous and tagines, and fragrant Berber desserts. The bar, Andy Wahloo, is a popular watering hole.

Auberge Pyrénées-Cévennes

106 rue de la Folie-Méricourt, 11th; tel: 01
43 57 33 78; closed Sun, most of Aug and
first week in Jan; metro: République; €€€

There's a reason why this classy spot won a best bistro award: the waiters are friendly, the decor is unique (purple-and-white cloths, terracotta floors, and stuffed animal heads on the wall), and the hearty food is top-notch. Try lentil caviar or *frisée aux lardons* (salad with bacon), followed by cassoulet, pigs' feet, fish *quenelles*, and rum Babas or profiteroles.

Bofinger

5–7 rue de la Bastille, 4th; tel: 01 42 72 87
82; daily noon–midnight; metro: Bastille;
€€€

Paris's oldest brasserie, which served the city's first draught beer in 1864 when phylloxera struck France's vineyards. Spectacular Belle Epoque interior: a revolving door, a glass domed ceiling, squishy leather bench seats and, upstairs, wall paintings of *kugelhof* and pretzels. The menu offers several kinds of *choucroute*, seafood, pigs' trotters and Paris-Brest. Good wines, many available by the glass.

Breizh Café

109 rue Vieille-du-Temple, 3rd; tel: 01 42 72
13 77; Wed–Sun 11.30am–11pm; metro:
Filles du Calvaire; €

Owned and run by a Breton, this popular crêperie offers a good selection of *galettes* (savoury buckwheat pancakes)

Dinnertime in Montmartre

and crêpes (sweet pancakes) made with organic flour. Try one with *andouille* (chitterling sausage) accompanied by a Breton cola or *lait ribot* (buttermilk). Vegetarians won't go hungry.

Le Dôme du Marais

53bis rue des Francs-Bourgeois, 4th; tel: 01 42 74 54 17; lunch and dinner daily; metro: Rambuteau; €€€

Unstuffy restaurant in a grand setting (once the auction house for the state-owned pawnbrokers). Beautifully executed seasonal market cuisine and a great place for Sunday brunch.

Georget

64 rue Vieille du Temple, 4th; tel: 01 42 78 55 89; Wed–Sun lunch, Tue–Sun dinner; metro: Saint-Paul; €€

Also known as Robert et Louise, this cosy restaurant with its roaring fire is a carnivore's delight: superb black pudding (accompanied by a lonely lettuce leaf), steak served on a wooden platter and thick, tasty beef stew.

Le Souk

1 rue Keller, 11th; tel: 01 49 29 05 08; closed Mon; metro: Ledru-Rollin; €€€

Excellent atmospheric Moroccan restaurant that serves up hearty, spiced cuisine. Choose from huge tagines, plentiful couscous plates and succulent lamb shanks followed by delicate pastries and end with a palate-cleansing mint tea. Plenty of vegetarian options and good-value lunch menus.

Latin Quarter/St-Germain

Le Comptoir

9 carrefour de l'Odéon, 6th; tel: 01 44 27 07 97; metro: Odéon; €€€

This gourmet bistro is one of the most desirable addresses in the area so book in advance. Next door, the more affordable Avant Comptoir offers wine by the glass as well as platters of charcuterie and other nibbles.

La Cuisine de Philippe

25 rue Servandoni, 6th; tel: 01 43 29 76 37; closed Sun and Mon; metro: St-Sulpice; €€€

Opposite the Jardin du Luxembourg, this charming little bistro serves traditional French dishes. Savoury and sweet soufflés are the house speciality.

Les Degrés de Notre-Dame

10 rue des Grands-Degrés, 5th; closed Sun; tel: 01 55 42 88 88; metro: Maubert-Mutualité; €

Tasty menu of bistro fare and Asian-inspired cuisine. A bargain.

La Fourmi Ailée

8 rue du Fouarre, 5th; tel: 01 43 29 40 99; open daily; metro: Maubert-Mutualité; €

Ambient, inexpensive, haven of a tea-room-cum-restaurant that was formerly a women's library (the walls are still lined with books).

Le Jardin des Pâtes

4 rue Lacépède, 5th; tel: 01 43 31 50 71; daily for lunch and dinner; metro: Place Monge; €€

St–Germain is foodie heaven

Ladurée macaroons are the perfect treat

Opposite the Jardin des Plantes, this little organic café specialises in pasta made from chestnut, rye, barley, buckwheat and more. A good option for vegetarians.

Le Timbre

3 rue Sainte-Beuve, 6th; tel: 01 45 49 10 40; www.restaurantletimbre.com; closed Sun, Mon and Aug; metro: Vavin, Notre-Dame-des-Champs; €€–€€€

Located near the Jardin du Luxembourg, in a vibrant, foodie-friendly area of the 6th dubbed the 'Quartier Vavin', British-born Christopher Wright's postage stamp-sized ('timbre' means stamp) eatery uses market-fresh produce to serve up French classics with an English twist. The well-executed set menu, costing around €26 per person and including service but not wine, has won rave reviews from critics in France and back across the Channel.

Montmartre

L'Annexe

13 rue des Trois Frères, 18th; tel: 01 46 06 12 48; Mon–Sat dinner only; metro: Abbesses; €€€

Cosy place run by two young women, one is the chef and the other is the sommelier, offering traditional French dishes including *tartare* (raw minced beef).

Chez Toinette

20 rue Germain-Pilon, 18th; tel: 01 42 54 44 36; Mon–Sat from 7.30pm; metro: Abbesses; €€€

Where many places in this part of town fob off unwitting tourists with overpriced fare, this amiable bistro has a good, well-priced blackboard menu that runs to steaks, wild-boar terrine, a lovely warm goat's cheese salad and prunes soaked in Armagnac.

Wepler

14 place de Clichy, 18th; tel: 01 45 22 53 24; daily 8am–12.30am; metro: Place de Clichy; €€€

Once a restaurant with a sideline as a billiards hall, now a brasserie with an emphasis on seafood. Indulge in a huge platter of oysters, whelks, clams, langoustines, crab and sea urchins.

The East and Northeast

Bistrot Paul Bert

18 rue Paul Bert, 11th; tel: 01 43 72 24 01; closed Sun, Mon and Aug; metro: Faidherbe-Chaligny; €€€

This bustling bistro is one of the best places in Paris to enjoy steak and chips. The menu is traditionally French, with a wide range of desserts including homemade raspberry *macarons* and the house speciality, a *Paris-Brest*. The wine menu is extensive, catering for all tastes and budgets, and a large number of wines are available by the glass.

Le Chapeau Melon

92 rue Rébeval, 19th; tel: 01 42 02 68 60; daily, food served Wed–Sun eve only; metro: Pyrénées; €–€€

Cooking with panache at La Coupole

Olivier Camus's Belleville restaurant, the 'Bowler Hat' – a former wine shop – now does a simple, no-choice three-course set menu in the evenings with a fabulous wine list, including some excellent organic bottles (quite a speciality here). Charming and friendly local restaurant.

Hermès

23 rue Mélingue, 19th; tel: 01 42 39 94 70; closed Sun, Mon; metro: Pyrénées; €€
Superb-value restaurant just south of the Parc des Buttes-Chaumont. Good food with a southwestern flavour.

Le Pavillon du Lac

Parc des Buttes Chaumont, 19th; tel: 01 42 00 07 21; Tue–Sat 10am–midnight, Sun until 8pm; metro: Buttes-Chaumont; €€€
Café-restaurant in a lovely setting next to the park's lake. Good-value set menus and Sunday brunch

Le Train Bleu

1st floor, Gare de Lyon, 12th, tel: 01 43 43 09 06; www.le-train-bleu.com; lunch and dinner daily; metro: Gare de Lyon; €€€€
In the midst of the Gare de Lyon, the terminus for trains from the Mediterranean, this huge, impressive brasserie was built for the 1900 World Fair. With its frescoed ceilings depicting destinations served by the trains from the station, mosaics and gilt detailing, it is Second Empire style at its very grandest. Classic French dishes are well prepared and efficiently served. Good-value set menus.

Le Verre Volé

67 rue de Lancry, 10th; tel: 01 48 03 17 34; open daily 9.30am–midnight; metro: Jacques Bonsergent; €€
This wine shop-cum-restaurant close to the Canal St-Martin is cosy inside, with cheery green wooden chairs and dinky tables packed together. Wine bottles line the walls – you can choose from a small number by the glass or else just pay a corkage charge on any of the 300 or so bottles for sale. The food is classic French fare.

Zoe Bouillon

66 rue Rébéval, 19th; tel: 01 42 02 02 83; Mon, Tue, Sat lunch only, Wed–Fri lunch and dinner, Sun dinner only; metro: Pyrénées; €
Healthy soups and salads are the specialities here. Great for vegetarians.

Western Paris

Chez Géraud

31 rue Vital, 16th; tel: 01 45 20 33 00; Mon–Fri; metro: La Muette; €€€
Classic bistro serving hearty regional cuisine, with the emphasis on roasted meat and game dishes. Excellent service.

Zebra Square

3 place Clément Ader, 16th; tel: 01 44 14 91 91; metro: Ranelagh; €€€
In Hotel Square, this stylish restaurant has a traditional menu with a nod towards the Mediterranean. Try the custardy *tarte tropézienne* for dessert.

Montparnasse and the New Left Bank

Chai 33

33 cour St-Emilion, 12th; tel: 01 53 44 01 01; open daily; metro: Cour St-Emilion; €€

Innovative restaurant in a former wine warehouse. Choose your wine from six styles, from light with a bite to rich and silky, with well-executed fusion food to match. Unpretentious sommeliers are on hand to help.

La Coupole

102 boulevard du Montparnasse, 14th; tel: 01 43 20 14 20; www.lacoupole-paris.com; daily 8.30am–midnight; metro: Vavin; €€€

This legendary Art Deco brasserie (the largest in Paris) opened its doors in 1927 and is still going strong. Now run by the Flo Brasserie group, it has a convivial atmosphere, and its popularity remains intact. The classic brasserie fare includes huge platters of shellfish, *choucroute* and Alsatian sausages, and steaks and hearty stews.

La Régalade

49 avenue Jean-Moulin, 14th; tel: 01 45 45 68 58; closed Sat, Sun, Mon lunch and Aug; metro: Alésia; €€€

A destination bistro for epicures across Paris for over 10 years, La Régalade never disappoints. Since taking over the reins, chef Bruno Doucet has injected it with life, while retaining much of what was good about it, especially the reasonable pricing. Start with the complementary *pâté de campagne* with 'rustic'

bread, then proceed with a cream of walnut soup poured over a flan of *foie gras*, duck hearts with oyster mushrooms, and Grand Marnier soufflé to finish. *Prix-fixe* menu is €34.

Yanasé

75 rue Vasco-de-Gama, 15th; tel: 01 42 50 07 20; closed Sun, Mon and Aug; metro: Lourmel; €€€€

More affordable than some of the Japanese restaurants around the Louvre (there's a lunch menu at €18), the quality is still high. The house speciality is *robata* (meat cooked on a charcoal grill) but traditionalists will also find sushi and sashimi. Green tea ice-cream is a good choice for dessert and if the weather's nice take out a bento box to eat in Parc André Citroën.

Outside Paris

Restaurant de la Maison Fournaise

Ile des Impressionistes, 3 rue du Bac, Chatou; tel: 01 30 71 41 91; €€€

This island makes a glorious spot for lunch or dinner, particularly in summer, on the lovely waterside terrace.

Gordon Ramsay au Trianon

Trianon Palace, 1 boulevard de la Reine, Versailles; tel: 01 30 84 55 55; Tue–Sat 8–10pm, Fri–Sat noon–2pm; €€€€

Set within the Trianon Palace hotel, on the edge of the palace grounds, is Gordon Ramsay's first fine-dining restaurant in France. A smart affair (no jeans or T-shirts).

Canal St-Martin in northeast Paris

NIGHTLIFE

Paris is legendary as a city of culture, with theatres, concert halls, cinemas, cabaret halls and clubs to suit every taste, housed in anything from an Art Deco palace to a Japanese pagoda.

Theatre

Comédie Française

1 place Colette, 1st; tel: 08 25 10 16 80 (from France)/033 1 44 58 15 15 (from outside France); www.comedie-francaise.fr; metro: Palais-Royal

Since 1799 France's national theatre has performed at this fine neoclassical building by the Palais Royal. Most productions are in the classical repertoire, by playwrights such as Corneille, Molière and Racine, although plays by more modern classic writers are also shown.

Odéon – Théâtre National de l'Europe

Place de l'Odéon, 5th; tel: 01 44 85 40 40; www.theatre-odeon.fr; metro: Odéon

This neoclassical behemoth stages classics, translations of foreign works, and contemporary drama – anything from Alexandre Dumas to new commissions.

Dance

Ballet de l'Opéra National de Paris

Bastille: 120 rue de Lyon, 12th; Palais-Garnier: Place de l'Opéra, 9th; tel: 08 92 89 90 90 (from within France)/+33 1 71 25 24 23 (from elsewhere); www.operadeparis.

fr; metro: Bastille (for the Opéra Bastille) or Opéra (for the Palais-Garnier)

Classics and new productions are staged by the Ballet de l'Opéra under current dance director Brigitte Lefèvre. Most are shown in the sumptuous 19th-century Palais Garnier (see page 44), although some are performed at the more modern Opéra Bastille (see page 55).

Théâtre National du Chaillot

Palais du Chaillot, 1 place du Trocadéro, 16th; tel: 01 53 65 30 00; www.theatre-chaillot.fr; metro: Trocadéro

This Art Deco complex houses three auditoria, mostly used for global dance performances, although also some drama.

Music

Caveau de la Huchette

5 rue de la Huchette, 5th; tel: 01 43 26 65 05; www.caveaudelahuchette.fr; metro: St-Michel

Established in 1946, this jazz and swing club was frequented by GIs during World War II and is still going strong, with big names such as Claude Bolling and Sacha Distel having performed here.

Opéra National de Paris, Bastille and Palais-Garnier

For details, see pages 55 and 44

The Opéra Bastille is the Opéra National's main venue for productions, with acclaimed conductor Philippe Jordan the

current Musical Director. Fans under 28 can enjoy cheap prices if they turn up on the day and there are still seats available.

Salle Pleyel

252 rue du Faubourg-St-Honoré, 8th; tel: 01 42 56 13 13; www.sallepleyel.fr; metro: Ternes

Built in 1927 by the piano makers after whom it is named, this concert hall with a fine Art Deco-style exterior is now home to the Orchestre de Paris. It mounts an excellent international programme of orchestral concerts and recitals.

Film

Le Balzac

1 rue Balzac, 8th; tel: 01 45 61 10 60; www.cinemabalzac.com; metro: George V

This stylish retro cinema shows the latest films as well as older films by season (silent movies, etc). Also hosts concerts.

Cinémathèque Française

51 rue de Bercy, 12th; tel: 01 71 19 33 33; www.cinemathequefrancaise.com; metro: Bercy

The headquarters of French cinema are based in a building designed by Frank Gehry. The Cinémathèque has a repertory cinema, a bookshop, restaurant, museum, research centre and archive.

Cabarets

Le Lido

116bis avenue des Champs-Élysées, 8th; tel: 01 40 76 56 10; www.lido.fr; metro: George V, Franklin D. Roosevelt

The famous 'Bluebell Girls' high-kick their way through the Lido's spectacular shows with countless costume changes, 23 sets and myriad special effects. Probably the grandest of the cabaret shows.

Moulin Rouge

82 boulevard de Clichy, 18th; tel: 01 53 09 82 82; www.moulinrouge.fr; metro: Blanche

Marvel at the 'Doriss' dancers as they parade in magnificent costumes dripping with feathers, sequins and rhinestones. You don't get much change from €100 (prices start at €99 for the show only) but it's crazily over the top and fun.

Clubs

Batofar

11 quai François-Mauriac, 13th; tel: 01 53 60 17 30; www.batofar.org; metro: Quai de la Gare

A lighthouse ship on the Seine that offers an alternative night out.

Bus Palladium

6 rue Pierre Fontaine, 18th; tel: 01 45 26 80 35; www.lebuspalladium.com; metro: Pigalle

Once frequented by Dali, Gainsbourg and The Beatles, it is now hip again

Le Rex Club

5 boulevard Poissonnière, 2nd; tel: 01 42 36 10 96; www.rexclub.com; metro: Bonne Nouvelle

A techno, house and drum 'n' bass stalwart, aimed more at hard-core clubbers than Parisian posers.

The Vélib' bike scheme is a real success

A–Z

A

Addresses

Paris is divided into 20 numbered districts, called *arrondissements* because they fan out in a 'round' pattern, clockwise from the city centre. Officially they are labelled by a five-digit postcode (75001, 75002, etc), but most people refer to them by their abbreviated form (1st, 2nd, 3rd, 4th, etc).

B

Bicycles

Some 23,000 bikes in around 1,700 racks across Paris can be used by anyone under the city's pioneering Vélib' (from 'vélo libre' or 'bike for free') scheme: www.velib.paris.fr. Simply swipe your credit card (some US cards may not work) or your Navigo Découverte travel card (see page 133), and pedal away. Depending on your usage, you will be charged either for one or seven days after the first half an hour, which is free.

Business hours

Traditionally, **banks** open from Monday to Friday 9am to 5.30pm and are closed at weekends. However, many now open on Saturday morning and close on Monday instead.

Most **boutiques** and **department stores** open between 9 and 10am, closing at around 7pm (later on Thursday). **Food shops**, especially bakers, open earlier. Lunchtime closing is increasingly rare; most shops do, however, close on Sunday, but bakers and patisseries usually open in the morning.

C

Climate

The average maximum in July and August is 25°C (77°F), the average minimum 15°C (59°F), but 27°C (81°F) is not unusual. In January, expect a maximum of 6°C (43°F), a minimum of 1°C (34°F).

Clothing

Paris is a great city to explore on foot, so comfortable walking shoes are essential. Bring warm clothes if you're visiting in winter, as the weather can be very chilly, and remember to have something waterproof (or at least an umbrella) with you in spring or autumn, as showers are quite common.

Size conversions

Women: 38 (UK 8/ US 6), 40 (UK 10/US 8), 42 (UK 12/US 10), etc. Men: suits: subtract 10, so a French 46 is equivalent to a UK or US 36. Shirts: 36 (14 UK/ US), 37 (141/2), 38 (15), etc.

Enjoying a fine day in the park

Crime and safety

In the event of loss or theft, a report must be reported in person at the nearest police station *(commissariat)* as soon as possible. See www.prefec-ture-police-paris.interieur.gouv.fr for addresses of stations; for emergency help tel: 17.

If you lose your passport, report it to your consulate straight after noti-fying the police. There is a list of con-sulates *(consulats)* in the local *Yellow Pages (Pages Jaunes)*, see www.pages jaunes.fr.

Security: It is advisable to take the same precautions in Paris as you would in any other capital city, notably watch-ing out for pickpockets on public trans-port and shielding your PIN at ATM machines. Keep a photocopy of your passport in case of theft. Known cen-tres of prostitution (such as Les Halles and parts of the Bois de Boulogne) are best avoided at night.

Customs regulations

Visitors of all nationalities must declare, upon arrival or departure, sums of cash exceeding €10,000 (or equivalent).

Duty-Paid Goods: If you are an EU resident and buy goods in France on which you pay tax, there are no restric-tions on the amounts you may take home with you. However, EU law has set 'guidance levels' on the amounts that are acceptable of the following, and if you exceed these amounts you must be able to show that the goods are for personal use:

Spirits: 10 litres

Fortified wine/wine: 90 litres (not more than 60 litres may be sparkling)

Beer: 110 litres.

Duty-Free Goods: If you are from out-side the EU and buy goods duty-free in France, the following limits still apply (these quantities may be doubled if you live outside Europe):

Tobacco: 200 cigarettes, or 100 ciga-rillos, or 50 cigars, or 250g of tobacco

Alcohol: 1 litre of spirits/liqueurs over 22 percent volume, or 2 litres under 22 percent. Four litres still wine and 16 litres beer

Perfume: 50g of perfume, plus 250ml of eau de toilette.

Disabled travellers

Travellers with mobility problems are advised to book accommodation in advance. Official hotel lists use a sym-bol to denote wheelchair access, but it's a good idea to check with the hotel regarding the exact facilities availa-ble. Information on hotels with good access facilities can be found on the Paris Tourist Office website, www.paris info.com.

Hotels in the Accor group (www.accor hotels.com) and Louvre Hotels group (www.louvrehotels.com) have at least one room for disabled guests in a vari-ety of chains to suit all budgets.

The two main French newspapers

French Organisations: Association des Paralysés de France, 13 place de Rungis, 13th; tel: 01 53 80 92 97; www.apf.asso.fr.

UK Organisations: Disability Rights UK, 12 City Forum, 250 City Road, London EC1V 8AF; tel: 020-7250 3222; www.disabilityrightsuk.org.

US Organisations: Society for Accessible Travel and Hospitality (SATH), 347 Fifth Avenue, Suite 605, New York; tel: 212-447 7284; www.sath.org.

E

Electricity

You will need an adaptor for most British and US plugs: French sockets have two round holes. Supplies are 230 volt, and US equipment needs a transformer.

Embassies/Consulates

Australia: 4 rue Jean-Rey, 15th; tel: 01 40 59 33 00.

Canada: 35 avenue Montaigne, 8th; tel: 01 44 43 29 00.

Republic of Ireland: *Embassy*: 12 avenue Foch, 16th; tel: 01 44 17 67 00.

UK: *Consulate*: 18bis rue d'Anjou, 8th; tel: 01 44 51 31 00.

US: *Embassy*: Consular Section, 4 avenue Gabriel, 1st; tel: 01 43 12 22 22.

Emergency numbers

Ambulance (SAMU): tel: 15
Fire brigade *(pompiers)*: tel: 18
Police *(police secours)*: tel: 17
From a mobile phone: tel: 112

G

Gay travellers

Although France has some way to go before gays have the same rights as heterosexuals, gays and lesbians are increasingly accepted in Paris, and this greater openness is being championed by the city's openly gay mayor Bertrand Delanoë. The Marais (4th *arrondissement*) is the most gay-friendly district. The annual Gay Pride March is held in June. The **Centre Lesbien, Gai, Bi et Trans**: (63 rue Beaubourg, 3rd; tel: 01 43 57 21 47) houses a lending library and advises on health, social and legal issues.

Gay/lesbian literature

There are various free magazines you can pick up in gay bars in the 3rd and 4th *arrondissements*. The magazine *Têtu* (www.tetu.com) is a useful source of information for the gay community, and can be bought at most news kiosks in the city. Also see www.legayparis.com and www.paris-gay.com.

Green issues

For information on environmental matters in Paris, visit the news section of www.environnement.paris.fr. When throwing away litter, note that white-lidded bins are for glass, yellow-lidded ones are for everything else recyclable and green bins are for non-recyclable rubbish.

Don't be distracted in Montmartre – be mindful of pickpockets.

H

Health

EU Nationals: If you are an EU national and you fall ill in France, you can receive emergency medical treatment from doctors, dentists and hospitals. You will have to pay the cost of this treatment, but are entitled to claim back up to 70 percent if you have a **European Health Insurance Card** (in the UK. tel: 0300 330 1350; www.ehic.org.uk).

North Americans: The International Association for Medical Assistance to Travellers (2162 Gordon Street, Ontario N1L 1G67, Canada; tel: 519-836 0102; www.iamat.org) is a non-profit-making group that offers members fixed rates for medical treatment, a medical record from their doctor and a directory of English-speaking doctors in France. Free membership.

American Hospital (Hôpital Américain de Paris): 63 boulevard Victor Hugo, Neuilly; tel: 01 46 41 25 25; www.american-hospital.org; metro: Porte Maillot, then bus 82 to the last stop. Private hospital with English-speaking staff.

Pharmacies

Most pharmacies are open from 9 or 10am to 7 or 8pm. At night, they post the addresses of the nearest late-opening pharmacies in their windows. Late-opening pharmacies include **Publicis Drugstore**, 133 avenue des Champs-Élysées,

8th; tel: 01 47 20 39 25; open daily 24 hrs; metro: Charles de Gaulle-Étoile.

I

Internet

WiFi (pronounced "wee-fee" in France) is now widely available in French hotels, although there is often a charge. For a list of free Wi-Fi spots around the city, including public buildings, parks and squares see www.paris.fr. A list of cafés with free Wi-Fi can be found here www.cafes-wifi.com. There are cyber cafés all over the city – ask at the tourist office for current ones or see www.parisinfo.com.

L

Lost property

To reclaim lost items in Paris, go in person (with ID) to the Bureau des Objets Trouvés, 36 rue des Morillons, 15th; tel: 08 21 00 25 25; Mon–Thu 8.30am–5pm, Fri 8.30am–4.30pm; metro: Convention.

M

Maps

Paris Classique par Arrondissement is similar to the London *A–Z* and can be bought for about €10 at newsstands.

Media

Newspapers: The two main national dailies are *Le Monde*, which has a rather dry and leftish slant, and the more con-

servative *Le Figaro*. On the far left is the Communist *L'Humanité*, while between that and *Le Monde* is Jean-Paul Sartre's brainchild, *Libération*.

The major weekly news magazines are *Le Point* (right), *L'Express* (centre) and *Le Nouvel Observateur* (left).

To find out what is going on in Paris, buy *L'Officiel des Spectacles* (out on Wednesday), with listings of films, clubs, exhibitions, concerts, theatres etc.

Radio: France Inter (87.8 MHz) is the biggest station, offering something to suit all tastes. Radio Classique (101.1 MHz) plays lightweight classical music. For something slightly less mainstream, try France Musiques (91.7 MHz), or RTL (104.3 MHz), which plays chart music interspersed with chat. Europe 1 (104.7 FM) is the best for morning news coverage, while France Info (105.5 FM) broadcasts the news.

Television: TF1, France 2, France 3, France 5/Arte and M6 are the five main television stations. There is also a huge choice of cable channels. Canal+ is a subscription channel, which shows big-name films.

Money

Currency: France uses the euro, divided into 100 cents. Coins *(pièces)* come in 1, 2, 5, 10, 20 and 50 cents, and 1 and 2 euros. Banknotes *(billets)* come in 5, 10, 20, 50, 100, 200 and 500 euros.

Exchange: Bureaux de change at train stations vary their hours in high or low seasons, but most are open Monday to Friday 7am–7pm. In banks, separate exchange counters are increasingly rare. Exchange offices at Roissy-Charles de Gaulle (terminals 2A, 2B and 2D) and Orly-Sud airports are open daily until 11pm. Travelex at 194 rue de Rivoli, 1st, tel: 01 47 03 49 52, or for other locations visit: www.travelex.fr. Mon-Sat 9.15am-7.30pm, Sun 10.45am-5.45pm. Multi Change at 180 boulevard St-Germain, 6th, tel: 01 42 22 41 00, www.multi-change.com. Mon-Sat 9.30am-6.30pm. Take your passport if you want to cash travellers' cheques.

Cash Machines: The easiest way to take out money is to use an ATM, with a debit or credit card such as Visa, MasterCard, Maestro or Cirrus, etc, and your PIN.

Credit Cards: Most shops, restaurants and hotels accept credit cards.

Post

Post Offices: Main branches are open Mon–Fri 8am–7pm, Sat 8am–noon. The central post office is at 52 rue du Louvre, 1st; www.laposte.fr.

Public holidays

1 Jan (New Year's Day)
Mar/Apr (Easter Monday)
1 May (Labour Day)
8 May (end of World War II in Europe)
Mid-/late May (Ascension Day)
Late May (Whit Monday)
14 July (Bastille Day)

Metro busker

15 Aug (Feast of the Assumption)
1 Nov (All Saints' Day)
11 Nov (Armistice Day, 1918)
25 Dec (Christmas)

 R

Religion

The majority of people in Paris are nominally Roman Catholic. The *Yellow Pages (Les Pages Jaunes)*, see www.pages-jaunes.fr, lists places of worship for every faith and denomination.

S

Smoking

In line with many other European countries, France has now banned smoking in railway stations, airports, shops and offices, restaurants and bars, with fines in place for anyone flouting the ban.

Stamps

These *(timbres)* are available at most *tabacs* (tobacconists) and other shops selling postcards or greetings cards. For more details and postage costs, visit www.laposte.fr.

T

Telephones

Phone Numbers: All telephone numbers in France have 10 digits. Paris and Île-de-France (Paris region) landline numbers begin with 01. Toll-free telephone numbers start 0800; all other numbers beginning 08 (accessible in France only) are charged at variable rates; 06 numbers are for mobile phones. For the operator, call 12.

Calling from Abroad: To dial Paris from the UK: 00 (international code) + 33 (France) + 1 (Paris) + an eight-figure number. To call other countries from France, dial the international code (00), then the country code: Australia 61, UK 44, US and Canada 1.

For US visitors, prepaid phonecards include ATT, Continental and Solaris: see www.comfi.com for details.

Public Telephone Boxes: Most phone boxes in Paris are operated with a card *(télécarte)*, bought from kiosks, *tabacs* and post offices. Cafés and *tabacs* often have public phones, which usually take coins or *jetons*, discs bought at the bar.

Time zones

France is one hour ahead of Greenwich Mean Time (GMT) and six ahead of Eastern Standard Time.

Tipping

By law, restaurant bills must include a service charge, which is usually 12 or 15 percent. Nevertheless, it is common to leave a small additional tip (not more than 5 percent) for the waiter if the service has been especially good. Address waiters as *Monsieur* (never *garçon*) and waitresses as *Mademoiselle,* if they are young, or *Madame,* if they are older.

For taxi fares, rounding up to the nearest euro is the norm.

Tour operators

By Boat: Seine cruises last an hour, with commentaries in several languages. In high season, boats leave every half-hour, 10am–10pm. **Batobus** is a 'riverbus' service based at Port de la Bourdonnais by the Eiffel Tower (tel: 08 25 05 01 01; www.batobus.com). **Bateaux Mouches** depart from Pont de l'Alma (tel: 01 42 25 96 10; www.bateaux-mouches.fr); **Vedettes du Pont Neuf** depart from Pont Neuf (tel: 01 46 33 98 38; www.vedettesdupontneuf.com).

Canal Trips: These run along the Canal St-Martin, from the Bastille to the Parc de la Villette and vice versa. Try **Canauxrama** (13 quai de la Loire, 19th; tel: 01 42 39 15 00; www.canauxrama.com) or **Paris Canal** (19–21 quai de la Loire, 19th; tel: 01 42 40 96 97; www.pariscanal.com).

By Coach: Most companies provide a commentary in several languages and pass the major sights, but do not stop along the way. **Les Cars Rouges** (English and French; tel: 01 53 95 39 53; www.carsrouges.com) runs double-decker buses to the main tourist sites. Hop off, sightsee, then catch a later bus. **Paris L'Open Tour** (tel: 01 42 66 56 56; www.parislopentour.com), operated by RATP, runs a similar service, also with open-topped double-decker buses.

By 2CV: **4 Roues sous 1 Parapluie** (22 rue Bernard, Dimey, 18th; tel: 0800 800 631 (free) or 06 67 32 26 68; www.4roues-sous-1parapluie.com) offers tours of the city in a soft-topped Citroën 2CV (hence the name: four wheels under an umbrella). Each car holds a maximum of three passengers.

Tourist information

In Paris: see http://en.parisinfo.com for details of all services. To call the Paris Tourist Office, tel: 08 92 68 30 00; calls cost €0.34 per minute. Branches include:
Main Branch: 25 rue des Pyramides, 1st; daily May–Oct 9am–7pm, Nov–Apr 10am–7pm; metro: Pyramides.
Gare de Lyon, 20 boulevard Diderot, 12th; Mon–Sat 8am–6pm; metro: Gare de Lyon.
Gare du Nord, 18 rue de Dunkerque, 10th; daily 8am–6pm; metro: Gare du Nord.
Anvers, 72 boulevard Rochechouart, 18th; daily 10am–6pm; metro: Anvers.
UK: Lincoln House, 300 High Holborn, London WC1V 7JH; tel: 0906 824 4123 (60p per min); http://uk.franceguide.com.
US: 825 3rd Avenue, 29 Fl, New York, NY 10022; tel: 212-745 0952; http://us.franceguide.com.
Canada: 1800 avenue McGill Collège, Bureau 1010, Montreal, Québec H3A 3J6; tel: 514-288 2026; http://ca.rendezvousfrance.com

Transport

Arrival

By Rail: Eurostar has fast, frequent rail services from London (St Pancras) or Ashford station to Paris (Gare du

Gridlock at the Arc de Triomphe

Nord). The service runs about 12 times a day and takes just over two hours (two hours from Ashford). For reservations, tel: 08432-186 186 (UK) or 08 92 35 35 39 (France) or visit www.eurostar. com. There are reduced fares for children aged 4–11; under 4s travel free but are not guaranteed a seat.

By Sea: Ferries running from the UK to northern France offer attractive prices in competition with the Channel Tunnel. There are motorway links from Boulogne, Calais and Le Havre to Paris.

By Air: Air France KLM is the main agent for flights to France from the US and within Europe. For British travellers, in addition to major airlines (British Airways, etc), several low-cost airlines including Easyjet, Ryanair and Flybe offer flights to Paris from London and other British cities. See www.skyscanner.net for the best deals.

By Car: Eurotunnel takes cars from Folkestone to Calais on the drive-on, drive-off **Le Shuttle**. It takes 35 minutes from platform to platform and about one hour from motorway to motorway. Payment is made at toll booths, which accept cash, cheques or credit cards. The price applies to the car, not the number of passengers.

You can book in advance with Eurotunnel on tel: 08443-353 535 (UK) or 08 10 63 03 04 (France) or at www. eurotunnel.com. You can also just turn up and take the next available service. Le Shuttle runs 24 hours a day,

and there are from two to five an hour, depending on the season and time.

By Bus: National Express Eurolines runs services daily from London's Victoria Coach Station to Paris, providing one of the cheaper ways to get there. Discounts are available for young people and senior citizens, and the ticket includes the ferry crossing. For details tel: 08717-818178; www.eurolines. co.uk; or Eurolines France, at the Gare Routière-Coach Station Galliéni, 28 avenue du Général de Gaulle, Bagnolet; tel: 08 92 89 90 91; metro Galliéni. See also www.eurolines.fr.

Airports

Roissy-Charles-de-Gaulle: The fastest way of getting to central Paris from Roissy-Charles-de-Gaulle is by RER B train. These leave every 15 minutes between around 5am and 11.45pm from terminal 2 and run to the metro at Gare du Nord or Châtelet. The journey takes around 50 minutes.

The **Roissy** bus runs between the airport and rue Scribe (near the Palais-Garnier) from terminals 1, 2 and 3. It runs every 15 minutes 6am–8.45pm, then every 20 minutes until 11pm. From the Palais-Garnier it runs from 5.45am–11pm, every 15–30 minutes. The **Air France bus** (to metro Porte de Maillot or Charles-de-Gaulle Étoile) runs every 15 minutes from 5.30am to 11pm.

By **taxi**, the journey from Charles de Gaulle can take anything from around 30 minutes to over an hour, depending

Tour group at the Louvre

on the traffic. The charge is metered, with supplements payable for each large piece of luggage. An average fare between the airport and central Paris is €50 by day, €60 at night.

Orly: To get to central Paris from Orly, take the **shuttle** from Orly Sud or Orly Ouest to Pont de Rungis railway station. The RER C stops at Austerlitz, Pont St-Michel and the Quai d'Orsay. It runs every 15 minutes from 5am to 12.50pm and takes around 30 minutes to Austerlitz.

Alternatively, the **Orlybus** (to place Denfert-Rochereau) leaves from Orly Sud or Orly Ouest. It runs every 15–20 minutes from 6am to 11.30pm. The costlier **Orlyval** automatic train is a shuttle to Antony (the nearest RER to Orly). It runs every 7 minutes, 6am–11pm, and takes 35 minutes.

Air France buses (to Invalides, Etoile and Gare Montparnasse) leave from Orly Sud or Orly Ouest. They run every 20 minutes from 5am to 11pm and take 30 minutes. Tickets are available on board. See also www.carsairfrance.com.

By **taxi**, the journey from Orly to the city centre takes around 20–40 minutes, depending on the traffic, and cost around €50.

Transport within Paris

Bus (autobus): Bus transport around Paris is efficient, though not always fast. You can get a bus map from metro station ticket offices. Most buses run 7am–8.30pm, some until 12.30am. Service is reduced on Sundays and public holidays. Some 47 Noctilien lines run from 12.30am–5.30am, with hubs at the Gare de l'Est, Gare Montparnasse, Gare St-Lazare, Châtelet and Gare de Lyon.

Tickets: You can buy a ticket as you board, but it's cheaper to buy a book of tickets *(carnet)* from any metro station or tobacconist. Bus and metro tickets are interchangeable. Punch your ticket in the validating machine when you get on. You can also buy special Paris Visite tourist passes or a Navigo Découverte swipe card *(see page 133)*.

Metro: The Paris Métropolitain is one of the most efficient and least expensive metro systems in the world. Services start at about 5.30am and finish around 1am. The RATP (metro organisation) has an information office at 54 quai de la Rapée, 12th; tel: 32 46 (within France); www.ratp.fr.

Express lines (RER – Réseau Express Régional) get you into the centre of Paris from the suburbs in about 15 minutes, with a few stops in between.

You can buy single tickets or you can get 10 journeys for the price of seven with a carnet (book) of tickets, also valid for the bus network and for the RER, provided that you stay within Paris and don't go to outer suburbs.

A **Paris Visite** ticket, valid for one, two, three or five days, for 1–3 or 1–6 zones (the latter includes airport links and travel to Disneyland Resort Paris and Versailles), allows unlimited travel on the bus, suburban trains, RER, trams

A car-free spot on the bank of the Seine

or metro, and reductions on entrance fees to various attractions. A day ticket, **Forfait 1 Jour Mobilis**, is valid for the metro, RER, buses, suburban trains and some airport buses.

For longer stays, the best buy is a Navigo Découverte swipe card. It costs from €5 for the card itself (and you'll need a passport photograph), which can then be topped up to make it into either a weekly (hebdomadaire) Mon–Sun, or monthly (mensuel) card – the latter dates from the first of the month. The Navigo card allows unlimited rides inside Paris on the metro, RER, suburban train, trams and buses.

Train: The SNCF (French Railways Authority) runs fast, comfortable trains on an efficient network. The high-speed service (TGV – *train à grande vitesse*). See www.sncf.com or www.voyages-sncf.com; tel: 36 35 (in France).

Taxi: An unoccupied cab can be recognised by an illuminated white sign on its roof. Fares differ according to the zones covered or the time of the day (you'll be charged more between 5pm and 7am and on Sunday), and there are extra charges for putting luggage in the boot and for pick-up at a station or airport. Taxi drivers can refuse to carry more than three passengers. The fourth, if admitted, pays a supplement.

The following taxi companies take phone bookings 24 hours a day:
Alpha: 01 45 85 85 85
G7: 36 07
Taxis Bleus: 36 09.

Car rental

To hire a car you will need to show your driving licence (held for at least a year) and passport. You will also need a major credit card, or a large deposit. The minimum age for renting cars is 21, although a young driver's supplement is usually payable for those under 25. Third-party insurance is compulsory, and full cover is recommended.

The international car-hire firms operating in Paris include: **Avis** (tel: 08 21 23 07 60; www.avis.fr), **Europcar/National/InterRent** (tel: 08 25 35 83 58; www.europcar.fr) and **Hertz** (tel: 01 39 38 38 38; www.hertz.fr).

Parking: Street parking is hard to find; spaces are usually controlled until 7pm by pay-and-display machines (horodateurs). Most car parks are underground (visit www.parkingsdeparis.fr).

Petrol (Gas): This can be hard to track down in the city centre, so if your tank is almost empty head for a *porte* (exit) on the Périphérique (the multi-lane ring road), where there are stations open 24 hours a day all year round.

Visas

All visitors to France require a valid passport. No visa is required by visitors from the EU, the US, Australia, Canada or New Zealand. Nationals of other countries may need a visa; if in doubt (and if visiting for over 90 days), check with the French Consulate in your home country.

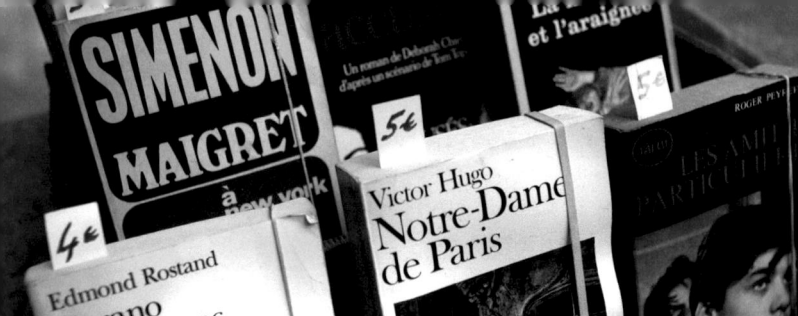

LANGUAGE

In general, if you attempt to communicate in French, the fact that you have made an effort is likely to break the ice and win favour with Parisians.

General

yes *oui*
no *non*
please *s'il vous plaît*
thank you (very much) *merci (beaucoup)*
you're welcome *de rien*
excuse me *excusez-moi*
hello *bonjour*
hi/bye *salut*
OK *d'accord*
goodbye *au revoir*
good evening *bonsoir*
How much is it? *C'est combien?*
What is your name? *Comment vous appelez-vous?*
My name is... *Je m'appelle...*
Do you speak English? *Parlez-vous anglais?*
I am English/American *Je suis anglais(e)/américain(e)*
I don't understand *Je ne comprends pas*
Please speak more slowly *Parlez plus lentement, s'il vous plaît*
Can you help me? *Pouvez-vous m'aider?*
I'm looking for... *Je cherche...*
Where is...? *Où est...?*
I'm sorry *Excusez-moi/Pardon*
I don't know *Je ne sais pas*
See you soon *A bientôt*
When? *Quand?*

What time is it? *Quelle heure est-il?*
here *ici*
there *là*
left *gauche*
right *droite*
straight on *tout droit*
far *loin*
near *près d'ici*
opposite *en face*
beside *à côté de*
today *aujourd'hui*
yesterday *hier*
tomorrow *demain*
now *maintenant*
later *plus tard*
this morning *ce matin*
this afternoon *cet après-midi*
this evening *ce soir*

Getting around

I want to get off at... *Je voudrais descendre à...*
Which line do I take for...? *Quelle ligne dois-je prendre pour...?*
Validate your ticket *Compostez votre billet*
airport *l'aéroport*
railway station *la gare*
bus station *la gare routière*
metro stop *la station de Métro*
bus *l'autobus, le car*
bus stop *l'arrêt*
platform *le quai*
ticket *le billet*
return ticket *aller-retour*

Two Left-Bank literary greats

Emergencies

Help! *Au secours!*
Stop! *Arrêtez!*
Where is the nearest telephone? *Où est le téléphone le plus proche?*
Where is the nearest hospital? *Où est l'hôpital le plus proche?*
I am sick *Je suis malade*
I have lost my passport/purse *J'ai perdu mon passeport/porte-monnaie*

Shopping

I'd like to buy *Je voudrais acheter*
How much is it? *C'est combien?*
Do you take credit cards? *Est-ce que vous acceptez les cartes de crédit?*
I'm just looking *Je regarde seulement*
size (clothes) *la taille*
size (shoes) *la pointure*
receipt *le reçu*

Sightseeing

tourist information office *l'office du tourisme*
free *gratuit*
open *ouvert*
closed *fermé*
every day *tous les jours*
to book *réserver*
town map *le plan*
road map *la carte*

Dining out

breakfast *le petit-déjeuner*
lunch *le déjeuner*
dinner *le dîner*
meal *le repas*
first course *l'entrée*

main course *le plat principal*
drink included *boisson comprise*
wine list *la carte des vins*
the bill *l'addition*
I am a vegetarian *Je suis végétarien(ne)*
I'd like to order *Je voudrais commander*
service included *service compris*

Online communications

Where's an internet cafe? *Où y-a-t-il un cyber café?*
Does it have wireless internet? *Est-ce qu'il a la connexion Wi-Fi?*
What is the WiFi password? *Quel est le mot de passe du WiFi?*
Is the WiFi free? *Est-ce que le WiFi est gratuit?*
Do you have bluetooth? *Avez-vous Bluetooth?*
Can I…? *Puis-je…?*
…access the internet *accéder à Internet*
…check my e-mail *consulter mes mails*
…print *imprimer*
…access Skype? *accéder à Skype?*
How much per half hour/hour? *Combien coûte la demi-heure/l'heure?*

Social Media

Are you on Facebook/Twitter? *Etes-vous sur Facebook/Twitter?*
What's your user name? *Quel est votre nom d'utilisateur ?*
I'll add you as a friend. *Je vous ajouterai comme ami.*
I'll put the pictures on Facebook/Twitter. *Je mettrai les photos sur Facebook/Twitter.*

BOOKS AND FILM

Books

François Villon's bawdy medieval poetry, the 19th-century realist novels of Victor Hugo or Honoré de Balzac, the Symbolist poetry of Charles Baudelaire and the Existentialist novels of Jean-Paul Sartre are just a few of the literary works that have taken inspiration from the city of Paris across the centuries.

History

A Concise History of France, by Roger Price. Excellent historical overview.

Marie Antoinette, by Antonia Fraser. An interesting biography of France's most famous queen.

Parisians: An Adventure History of Paris, by Graham Robb. A fascinating look at the individuals who shaped the city.

Sylvia Beach and the Lost Generation: A History of Literary Paris in the Twenties and Thirties, by Noel Riley Fitch. The origins of Shakespeare & Company bookshop and the writers who went there.

Art and architecture

A Propos de Paris, by Henri Cartier-Bresson. Some 130 stunning black-and-white photographs of the capital, spanning 50 years.

The Cathedral Builders, by Jean Gimpel. The story of the hands and minds behind the cathedrals of France.

Paris: An Architectural History, by Anthony Sutcliffe. A great book on the architecture of the capital across the ages.

Paris: Art and Architecture by Martina Padberg. A comprehensive guide to the city's art and architecture from its origins to the 21st century.

Robert Doisneau: Paris. A compact book featuring more than 600 of the photographer's images of Paris.

Expat memoirs

A Moveable Feast, by Ernest Hemingway. Life with the literati in 1920s Paris.

A Year in the Merde, by Stephen Clarke. The best-selling humorous tale of an expat in Paris.

Fiction

Murder in the Palais Royal, by Cara Black. One of a series of entertaining crime novels set in and around Paris.

The Elegance of the Hedgehog, by Muriel Barbery. A moving tale of a friendship between a young girl and the concierge of her apartment building.

The Sun King Rises, by Yves Jégo and Denis Lépée. Intrigue and mystery in the court of Louis XIV.

Food

Paris Bistro Cooking, by Linda Dannenberg. Tasty dishes from a wealth of Paris brasseries.

The Little Paris Kitchen, by Rachel Khoo.

Paris has inspired countless books and films

Easy-to-make versions of French classics. **The Paris Café Cookbook**, by Daniel Young. Recipes and excerpts on recommended cafés in the capital.

The Sweet Life in Paris, by David Lebovitz. The Paris-based American chef's observations on Paris and cooking, including 50 recipes.

Films

If Paris feels eternally familiar, thank the movies. Indeed, you're in film-set Paris the second you get off the train at the Gare du Nord, filmed by Orson Welles **(F for Fake)**, amongst many others.

Next, naturally, you make your way to the Métro – an even more popular film location, used by everyone from Henri-Georges Clouzot to the Coen brothers. Perhaps you come out at the Champs-Elysées – another classic setting; as you walk up, imagine the Wehrmacht's daily parade coming the other way, as recreated to sobering effect in Jean-Pierre Melville's **L'Armée des Ombres** (1969). Or retrace Jean Seberg and Jean-Paul Belmondo's steps as they walk down the famous avenue in probably the most famous Paris film, Jean-Luc Godard's **Breathless** (**A Bout de Souffle**; 1960).

And it's hard to miss the Eiffel Tower: not only filmed more times than it has rivets (the pioneering Lumière brothers were first – their 1900 portrait of the 11-year-old tower is still extant), it even starred in its own cartoon, **Bonjour Paris**.

Hollywood has long been enchanted by the City of Light, from the 1950s films **An American in Paris**, starring Gene Kelly, and **Funny Face**, featuring Audrey Hepburn, to the controversial 1970s Marlon Brando movie **Last Tango in Paris** and Woody Allen's time-travelling 2011 offering, **Midnight in Paris**. And the 2006 anthology **Paris, je t'aime (Paris, I love you)**, featuring a flurry of European and Hollywood actors, is made up of 22 short films each set in a different *arrondissement*.

For a slice of the gritty life in the *banlieues* that surround Paris, Matthieu Kassovitz's ferocious 1995 agitprop drama **La Haine** (1995) is still all too relevant. At the other end of the spectrum is Jean-Pierre Jeunet's 2001 smash hit **Amélie (Le Fabuleux Destin d'Amélie Poulain)**, a sugary-sweet nostalgic tale of villagey Paris.

New Wave

When people think of Paris movies, they often have in mind a small clutch of films –including **Breathless** and **The 400 Blows** – made by a small group of people in a short space of time. These Nouvelle Vague ("new wave") films were made between the late 1950s and mid-1960s, by a loosely affiliated group of directors opposed to what they saw as the stuffiness of cinema of the day; its leading figures were Jean-Luc Godard, François Truffaut, Claude Chabrol, Eric Rohmer and Jacques Rivette. One of the movement's few women directors was Agnès Varda, whose 1962 film **Cléo de 5 à 7** is one of the best of the bunch.

ABOUT THIS BOOK

This *Explore Guide* has been produced by the editors of Insight Guides, whose books have set the standard for visual travel guides since 1970. With top-quality photography and authoritative recommendations, these guidebooks bring you the very best routes and itineraries in the world's most exciting destinations.

BEST ROUTES

The routes in the book provide something to suit all budgets, tastes and trip lengths. As well as covering the destination's many classic attractions, the itineraries track lesser-known sights, and there are also excursions for those who want to extend their visit outside the city. The routes embrace a range of interests, so whether you are an art fan, a gourmet, a history buff or have kids to entertain, you will find an option to suit.

We recommend reading the whole of a route before setting out. This should help you to familiarise yourself with it and enable you to plan where to stop for refreshments – options are shown in the 'Food and Drink' box at the end of each tour.

For our pick of the tours by theme, consult Recommended Routes for... (see pages 4–5).

INTRODUCTION

The routes are set in context by this introductory section, giving an overview of the destination to set the scene, plus background information on food and drink, shopping and more, while a succinct history timeline highlights the key events over the centuries.

DIRECTORY

Also supporting the routes is a Directory chapter, with a clearly organised A–Z of practical information, our pick of where to stay while you are there and select restaurant listings; these eateries complement the more low-key cafés and restaurants that feature within the routes and are intended to offer a wider choice for evening dining. Also included here are some nightlife listings, plus a handy language guide and our recommendations for books and films about the destination.

ABOUT THE AUTHORS

Victoria Trott is a freelance travel writer who specialises in France. A graduate in French and Spanish from Leeds University, she contributes to a wide variety of publications and has written or updated guidebooks for most major travel publishers. Her first visit to Paris didn't go too well: it rained every day and she got lost every time she used the metro. However, after being seduced by cake shops and the bygone charm of the Latin Quarter, Paris is now her favourite city.

This book builds on original content by Michael Macaroon.

CONTACTING EDITORS

We would appreciate it if readers would alert us to errors or outdated information by writing to us at insight@apaguide.co.uk or APA Publications, PO Box 7910, London SE1 1WE, UK.

CREDITS

Explore Paris
Contributors: Victoria Trott, Michael Macaroon
Commissioning Editor: Carine Tracanelli
Series Editor: Sarah Clark
Art Editor: Alice Earle
Map Production: Berndtson Gmbh, updated by Apa Cartography Department
Production: Tynan Dean and Rebeka Davies

Photo credits: Alamy 70, 80, 81, 82, 84L, 85, 88; Apa Publications 4MC, 42/43, 84/85, 96L, 97; Art Archive 33L; Bridgeman Art Library 20, 90L, 96/97; Britta Jaschinski/Apa Publications 104; Corbis 21; Disneyland Paris 98, 98/99, 99L; Fotolia 94; Getty Images 40, 74, 75, 79L, 89; Ilpo Musto/Apa Publications 1, 2MC, 4TL, 11, 12T, 12B, 32, 58, 63, 69, 77L, 78/79, 91, 92, 93, 118L, 127, 133; iStockphoto 95; Kevin Cummins/Apa Publications 2ML, 2MC, 2MR, 2MR, 2ML, 2/3T, 5T, 6ML, 6ML, 6MC, 6MC, 6MR, 6MR, 10, 22ML, 22MC, 22ML, 22MR, 29, 43, 49, 53, 59, 61, 62L, 72, 73L, 72/73, 78, 83, 90/91, 100ML, 100MC, 100MR, 100MR, 100MC, 100ML, 100/101T, 102/103, 107, 123, 124, 125, 126, 128, 129, 130/131, 132, 134, 135; LHW 104/105; Ming Tang-Evans/Apa Publications 4ML, 4BC, 5MR, 5M, 5MR, 6/7T, 8, 9, 13, 14L, 14/15, 15, 16, 16/17, 17L, 18, 19, 22MR, 22MC, 22/23T, 24, 25, 26, 27, 28, 30, 31L, 30/31, 32/33, 34, 35, 36L, 36/37, 37, 38L, 38/39, 39, 41, 42L, 44L, 44/45, 45, 46, 47, 48, 50, 51, 52L, 52/53, 54, 55, 56, 57, 60, 61L, 62/63, 64L, 64/65, 65, 66, 66/67, 67L, 68L, 68/69, 71, 76, 76/77, 86L, 86/87, 87, 105L, 108/109, 110/111, 112, 112/113, 113L, 114, 115, 116, 116/117, 117L, 118/119, 119, 120, 121, 122, 136/137; Terrass 106
Cover credits: Front Cover Main: Eiffel Tower, *Corbis*
Front Cover BL: baguettes, *Kevin Cummins/Apa Publications*
Back Cover: (Left) View from Institut du Monde Arabe *Ming Tang-Evans/Apa* (Right): Moulin Rouge *Ilpo Musto/Apa*

Printed by CTPS – China

DISTRIBUTION

Worldwide
APA Publications GmbH & Co. Verlag KG (Singapore branch)
7030 Ang Mo Kio Ave 5, 08-65
Northstar @ AMK, Singapore 569880
Email: apasin@singnet.com.sg
UK and Ireland
Dorling Kindersley Ltd (a Penguin Company)
80 Strand, London, WC2R 0RL, UK
Email: customerservice@uk.dk.com
US
Ingram Publisher Services
One Ingram Blvd, PO Box 3006, La Vergne, TN 37086-1986
Email: ips@ingramcontent.com
Australia
Universal Publishers
PO Box 307, St. Leonards NSW 1590
Email: sales@universalpublishers.com.au
New Zealand
Brown Knows Publications
11 Artesia Close, Shamrock Park, Auckland, New Zealand 2016
Email: sales@brownknows.co.nz

INDEX

MAP LEGEND

● Start of tour

→ Tour & route direction

❶ Recommended sight

❷ Recommended restaurant/café

★ Place of interest
❶ Tourist information
Ⓜ ⓇⒺⓇ Metro / RER station
🛈 Statue/monument
✉ Main post office
🚌 Main bus station
--- Ferry route
═══ National park boundry
▬▬ Regional boundary

Park

Important building

Hotel

Transport hub

Shopping / market

Pedestrian area

Urban area

Marsh

INSIGHT GUIDES

INSPIRING YOUR NEXT ADVENTURE

Insight Guides offers you a range of travel guides to match your needs. Whether you are looking for inspiration for planning a trip, cultural information, walks and tours, great listings, or practical advice, we have a product to suit you.